aftermath

DALE SEYMOUR

Palo Alto,
California

MARY LAYCOCK
Nueva Learning
Center
Hillsborough,
Calif.

VERDA HOLMBERG
Mt. Diablo U.S.D.
Concord,
Calif.

BOB
LARSEN
Cartoonist

Ruth
HELLER
Designer

ISBN: 0-88488-035-4

7 8 9 10 11 12 . 8 9 8 7 6 5 4

A PUZZLE PAGE FOR TEACHERS

WHAT IS THE ANSWER TO THESE QUESTIONS?*

* TO FIND THE ANSWER, ORDER THE LETTERS BY THE QUESTIONS TO FORM ONE WORD.

OKAY...NOW HOW DO I AFTERMATH?

DEDICATION:

THIS BOOK IS DEDICATED TO COL. ROBERT S. BEARD. HIS INSIGHTS INTO THE BEAUTY OF MATHEMATICS HAVE BEEN A GREAT INSPIRATION TO THE AUTHORS OF THIS BOOK AS WELL AS MANY OTHERS.

ACKNOWLEDGEMENTS:

JUDY WILLIAMSON

REUBEN SCHADLER

DENNIS HOLMAN

CAROL CASHIN

FRAN WUNDER

FRED HORNBRUCH

BILL JUAREZ

CELEBRATION
TODAY
at
NUMBERS PARK

TWO NEW STATUES
TO BE DONATED

FELLOW NUMBERS, WE ARE GATHERED HERE TODAY TO HONOR TWO VERY SPECIAL MEMBERS OF OUR GROUP.

THE FIRST STATUE I AM GOING TO UNVEIL IS A NUMBER THAT IS VERY DEAR TO US.

A NUMBER THAT IS A FACTOR OF EVERY ONE OF US...

A DIVISOR OF EVERY ONE OF US.....

THAT MEANS IT DIVIDES US WITHOUT A REMAINDER.

OH!

LIKE MANY OF US, THIS NUMBER HAS MANY NAMES, BUT ITS MANY NAMES ARE MOST USEFUL IN HELPING TO ADD AND SUBTRACT FRACTIONS.

ALTHOUGH THIS NUMBER IS THE LEAST OF A SPECIAL GROUP OF US, IT CAN BE USED TO PROVE THERE IS NO BIGGEST ONE OF US.

MINUTES LATER...

THAT 3 MAY BE TALKING ALL NIGHT. DO YOU KNOW WHAT NUMBER HE IS TALKING ABOUT?

BLAH! BLAH!

SURE! DON'T YOU?

YOU WERE RIGHT, THE NUMBER WAS 1. IT HAS MANY SPECIAL AND USEFUL PROPERTIES.

I WONDER WHAT THE OTHER NUMBER IS.

AND NOW FOR OUR SECOND HONORED NUMBER.

WHENEVER THIS NUMBER IS ADDED TO ONE OF US, WE DO NOT CHANGE AT ALL.

THIS NUMBER OFTEN ACTS AS A REFEREE BY SEPARATING THE POSITIVES AND THE NEGATIVES.

WHAT OTHER NUMBER CAN CHANGE ONE TO A MILLION?

THIS FELLOW NUMBER OF OURS CAN CHANGE ANY ONE OF US INTO ITSELF BY MERELY MULTIPLYING ITSELF TIMES US.

FOR MY NEXT TRICK!

CAN YOU FIGURE OUT WHICH NUMBER IS BEING HONORED?

NAUGHT ME.

IT DOESN'T ADD UP.

STAR SEARCH

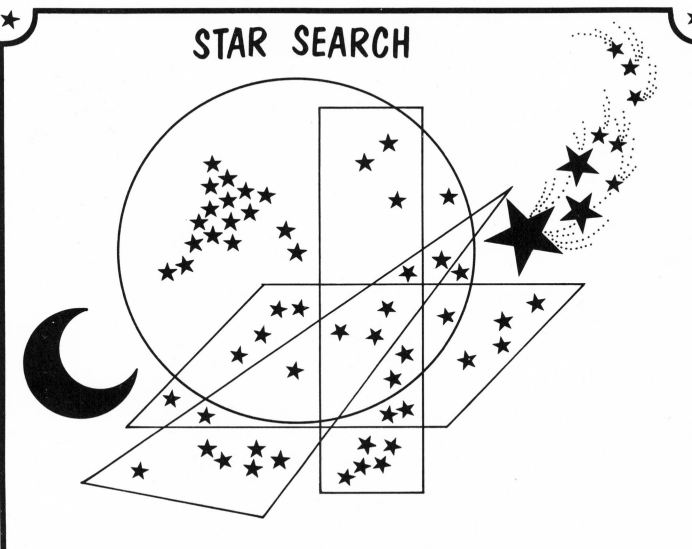

HOW MANY STARS ARE THERE

_____ 1) IN THE ▭ BUT NOT IN THE ◯ , △ OR ▱ ?

_____ 2) IN THE ◯ BUT NOT IN THE ▭ , △ OR ▱ ?

_____ 3) COMMON TO THE △ AND ▱ BUT NOT IN ◯ OR ▭ ?

_____ 4) COMMON TO THE ◯ AND ▱ BUT NOT IN THE △ OR ▭ ?

_____ 5) COMMON TO THE ◯ , ▭ AND ▱ BUT NOT IN THE △ ?

_____ 6) COMMON TO THE ▭ AND ◯ BUT NOT IN THE △ OR ▱ ?

_____ 7) COMMON TO THE △ , ▭ AND ▱ BUT NOT IN THE ◯ ?

_____ 8) COMMON TO THE ◯ , △ AND ▱ BUT NOT IN THE ▭ ?

_____ 9) COMMON TO THE ◯ , ▭ AND △ BUT NOT IN THE ▱ ?

_____ 10) COMMON TO ALL FOUR FIGURES?

MULTIBASE CHART

YOU CAN USE THE TABLE AND SLIDE BELOW TO MAKE A COUNTING CHART IN BASES **TWO** THROUGH **TEN**. CUT OUT THE SLIDE BELOW OR MAKE ONE LIKE IT. I WILL SHOW YOU HOW IT IS USED ON THE NEXT PAGE.

H	90	91	92	93	94	95	96	97	98	99
G	80	81	82	83	84	85	86	87	88	89
F	70	71	72	73	74	75	76	77	78	79
E	60	61	62	63	64	65	66	67	68	69
D	50	51	52	53	54	55	56	57	58	59
C	40	41	42	43	44	45	46	47	48	49
B	30	31	32	33	34	35	36	37	38	39
A	20	21	22	23	24	25	26	27	28	29
	10	11	12	13	14	15	16	17	18	19
	0	1	2	3	4	5	6	7	8	9
			A	B	C	D	E	F	G	H

SLIDE

CONTINUED

4

MULTIBASE CHART

IF I PLACE MY SLIDE OVER ROW **C**, I HAVE A **BASE FOUR** CHART. IN BASE FOUR, WE COUNT 1, 2, 3, 10, 11, 12, 13, 20 21, ...
TELL WHAT BASE CHARTS ARE REPRESENTED BELOW.

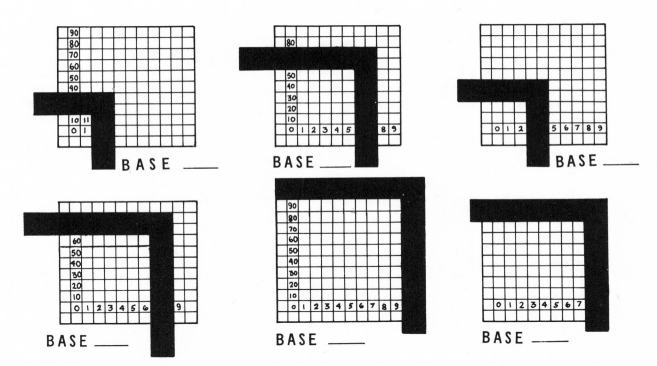

BASE _____

BASE _____

BASE _____

BASE _____

BASE _____

BASE _____

USE THE COUNTING CHART ON THE PRECEDING PAGE TO:

1) LIST MULTIPLES OF TWO IN A GIVEN BASE
2) LIST THE EVEN NUMBERS IN AN ODD BASE
3) WRITE AN ADDITION TABLE IN A GIVEN BASE

DESIGN MATRIX PUZZLE

CUT OUT THE SIX SECTIONS BELOW AND REARRANGE
THEM SO THAT THE SAME DESIGN DOES NOT APPEAR
TWICE IN THE SAME COLUMN, ROW OR DIAGONAL.

6

UNSCRAMBLE THE SIX MATH WORDS BELOW, WRITING EACH IN ITS SPECIAL BOX. TRANSFER THE LETTERS IN THE NUMBERED SQUARES TO THE BLANKS IN THE JOKE AT THE RIGHT. (ALL WORDS ARE ABOUT MEASUREMENT!)

MATH PUN FUN!

RAAE

| | | 1 | | |

UMEOLV

| | | | | 2 | |

THELNG

| | 3 | | | | |

TEERM

| | | | | 5 |

NISEHC

| | | | | | 4 |

REEMSUA

| | | | 6 | | |

THE DECODED WORD IS THE **KEY** WORD IN THIS MATH PUN!

WHAT DO A KING AND A FOOT HAVE IN COMMON?

THEY ARE BOTH...

‾ ‾ ‾ ‾ ‾ ‾
1 2 3 4 5 6

UNIT-WIT!

7

ADD-SUB SLIDE RULE

(OTHER BASES)

HERE IS A SLIDE RULE YOU CAN
MAKE TO HELP YOU ADD AND SUB-
TRACT NUMBERS IN OTHER BASES.

FIRST: CUT OUT SLIDE A AND FOLDER B.

0	1	2	3	4	5	6	10	11	12	13	14	15	16	20

ADD-SUB BASE 7   SLIDE A

0	1	2	3	4	5	6	10	11	12	13	14	15	16	20

- -

FOLD ON DOTTED LINE

FOLDER B

SECOND: FOLD BACK FOLDER B ON THE DOTTED LINE.

THIRD: PLACE SLIDE A INSIDE FOLDER B.   THE NUMBER
LINE A APPEARS BENEATH THE NUMBER LINE ON B.

PROBLEM: $4_7 + 5_7 = N$

1. PULL SLIDE A UNTIL 0
   IS OVER 4, ON FOLDER B.
2. ON A FIND 5_7.   THE
   ANSWER, N IS UNDER 5.

$N = \underline{\quad}_7$

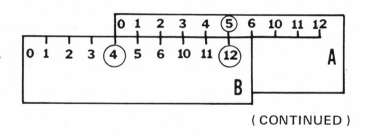

(CONTINUED)

8

ADD-SUB SLIDE RULE

(OTHER BASES)

CAN YOU WORK THESE BASE SEVEN ADDITION PROBLEMS USING THE **ADD-SUB** SLIDE RULE YOU MADE ON THE PREVIOUS PAGE?

1) $3_7 + 2_7 = N$ 5) $4_7 + 11_7 = N$

2) $4_7 + 3_7 = N$ 6) $12_7 + 3_7 = N$

3) $2_7 + 6_7 = N$ 7) $6_7 + 6_7 = N$

4) $5_7 + 0_7 = N$ 8) $10_7 + 10_7 = N$

SUBTRACTING

PROBLEM: $11_7 - 5_7 = N$

1. PULL SLIDE A UNTIL 0 IS OVER 5_7 ON B.

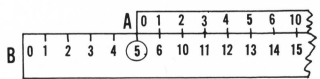

2. THINK $5_7 + N = 11_7$ YOUR ANSWER IS DIRECTLY ABOVE 11_7 ON SLIDE A.

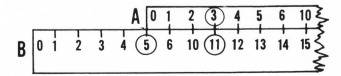

TRY THESE SUBTRACTION PROBLEMS ON THE ADD-SUB SLIDE RULE.

9) $5_7 - 2_7 = N$

10) $4_7 - 3_7 = N$

11) $10_7 - 4_7 = N$

12) $13_7 - 4_7 = N$

13) $20_7 - 11_7 = N$

14) $16_7 - 6_7 = N$

(CONTINUED)

ADD-SUB SLIDE RULE
(OTHER BASES)

CUT OUT THIS ADD–SUB SLIDE RULE
AND USE IT AS SHOWN ON PREVIOUS
PAGES TO COMPLETE THE ADDITION
TABLE BELOW:

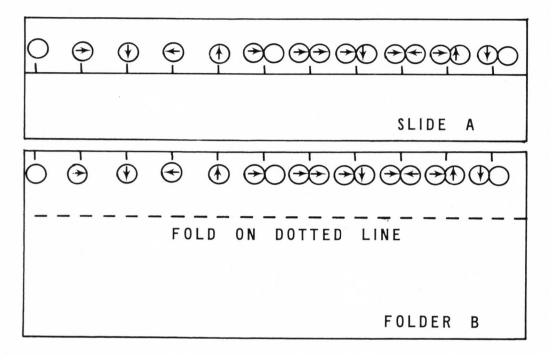

SLIDE A

FOLD ON DOTTED LINE

FOLDER B

ADDITION
TABLE.

MOVING MATCHES

I. MOVE TWO OF THESE MATCHES AND ADD ONE MORE TO FORM TWO DIAMONDS.

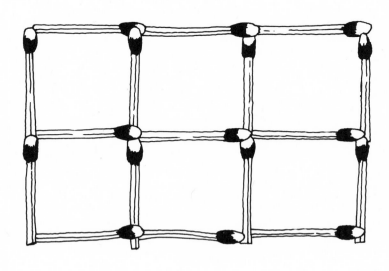

II. MOVE ONE MATCH TO FORM A TRUE EQUATION.

III. 17 MATCHES, 6 SQUARES: REMOVE FIVE MATCHES TO LEAVE THREE SQUARES THE SAME SIZE AND SHAPE AS THE ORIGINAL SIX.

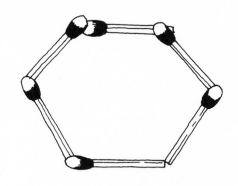

IV. 15 MATCH GAME:

TWO PEOPLE PLAY THIS GAME. LAY·OUT 15 MATCHES. PLAYERS TAKE TURNS. DURING A TURN, A PLAYER TAKES EITHER. ONE, TWO, OR THREE MATCHES. THE ONE WHO IS LEFT WITH THE LAST MATCH IS THE LOSER.

DON'T BE A POOR LOSER.

11

DIVISIBILITY

HERE ARE SOME MORE TESTS FOR DIVISIBILITY.

32

8

A NUMBER IS DIVISIBLE BY EIGHT IF:

THE LAST THREE DIGITS ARE DIVISIBLE BY EIGHT.

79365**800** THAT IS!

9

A NUMBER IS DIVISIBLE BY NINE IF THE SUM OF ITS DIGITS IS DIVISIBLE BY NINE.

2754
$2 + 7 + 5 + 4 = 18$
$18 \div 9 = 2$

2754 IS DIVISIBLE BY NINE.

10

A NUMBER IS DIVISIBLE BY TEN IF IT ENDS IN ZERO.

YOU **OUGHT** TO KNOW THAT!

12

A NUMBER IS DIVISIBLE BY TWELVE IF IT IS DIVISIBLE BY THREE AND FOUR.

DO YOU RECALL THE TESTS FOR 3 + 4!

CIRCLE IF DIVISIBLE BY:

a. 45600   8 9 10 12
b. 100000   8 9 10 12
c. 202008   8 9 10 12
d. 12121212   8 9 10 12
e. 300300300   8 9 10 12
f. 7500   8 9 10 12
g. 900090   8 9 10 12
h. 123456789   8 9 10 12

DIJAKNOWTHAT

A PIPE WITH A TWO INCH DIAMETER WILL CARRY
FOUR TIMES AS MUCH WATER AS A PIPE WITH
A ONE INCH DIAMETER?

THERE ARE ONLY FIVE SQUARES IN THIS CIRCLE?

THERE ARE ONLY 16 PRIME PALINDROMIC NUMBERS
LESS THAN 1000? (EXAMPLE: 11, 101, 131, 727).

$$9 \cdot 9 = 81$$
$$99 \cdot 99 = 9801$$
$$999 \cdot 999 = 998001$$
$$9999 \cdot 9999 = 99980001$$
$$99999 \cdot 99999 = 9999800001$$
$$999999 \cdot 999999 = 999998000001$$
$$9999999 \cdot 9999999 = \underline{\hspace{4cm}}$$

13

ARROWMATH
AND
INVERSE OPERATIONS

HERE ARE SOME EXAMPLES OF
INVERSE OPERATIONS:

UNTYING IS THE INVERSE OF TYING.

UNBUTTONING IS THE INVERSE OF
BUTTONING.

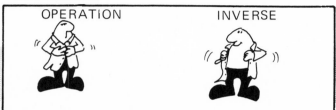

SUBTRACTION IS THE INVERSE OF
ADDITION.

OPERATION	INVERSE
$2 + 3 = 5$	$5 - 3 = 2$

DIVISION IS THE INVERSE OF
MULTIPLICATION.

OPERATION	INVERSE
$4 \times 7 = 28$	$28 \div 4 = 7$

QUESTIONS FOR DISCUSSION:

1. DOES CLIMBING A TREE HAVE AN INVERSE?

2. DOES MOWING THE LAWN HAVE AN INVERSE?

3. WHAT IS THE INVERSE OF SUBTRACTION? _____

4. WHAT IS THE INVERSE OF DIVISION? _____

(CONTINUED)

ARROWMATH AND INVERSES

EXAMPLES:

$1 \rightarrow = 2$

$1 \rightarrow \rightarrow = 3$

$1 \rightarrow \downarrow = 7$

1	2	3	4	5
6	7	8	9	10
11	12	13	14	15
16	17	18	19	20

SOLVE:

① $6 \rightarrow$ = _____

② $8 \downarrow \rightarrow$ = _____

③ $9 \nearrow \downarrow$ = _____

④ $13 \searrow \uparrow$ = _____

⑤ $16 \nearrow \nearrow \nearrow$ = _____

⑥ $7 \rightarrow \leftarrow$ = _____

⑦ $12 \nearrow \nearrow$ = _____

⑧ $18 \uparrow \downarrow$ = _____

INVERSE MEANS TO UNDO WHAT YOU JUST DID.

WHAT ARE THE INVERSES OF THESE **ARROWMATH** OPERATIONS?

⑨ $\rightarrow$ _____ INVERSE

⑩ $\uparrow$ _____ INVERSE

⑪ $\nearrow$ _____ INVERSE

⑫ $\nwarrow$ _____ INVERSE

⑬ $\leftarrow$ _____ INVERSE

HOW MANY?

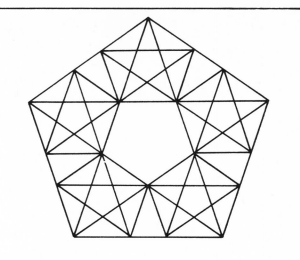

HOW MANY REGULAR PENTAGONS? _____

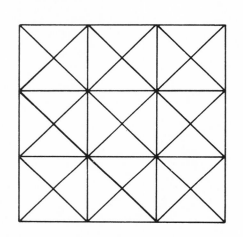

HOW MANY SQUARES? _____

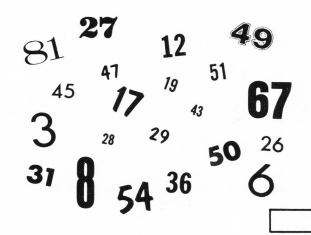

HOW MANY COMPOSITE NUMBERS?

HOW MANY THREE LETTER LICENSE PLATES CAN BE MADE USING THE LETTERS A, B, AND C ? _____

MONEY MATCHING

CAN YOU MATCH THESE FAMOUS AMERICAN FACES AND THE DENOMINATION ON WHICH THEIR PORTRAIT APPEARS?

JACKSON

HAMILTON

LINCOLN

FRANKLIN

WASHINGTON

JEFFERSON

GRANT

1 ONE 1 _____

2 - 2 _____

5 5 _____

10 10 _____

20 20 _____

50 50 _____

100 100 _____

17

MULTIPLE MAGIC

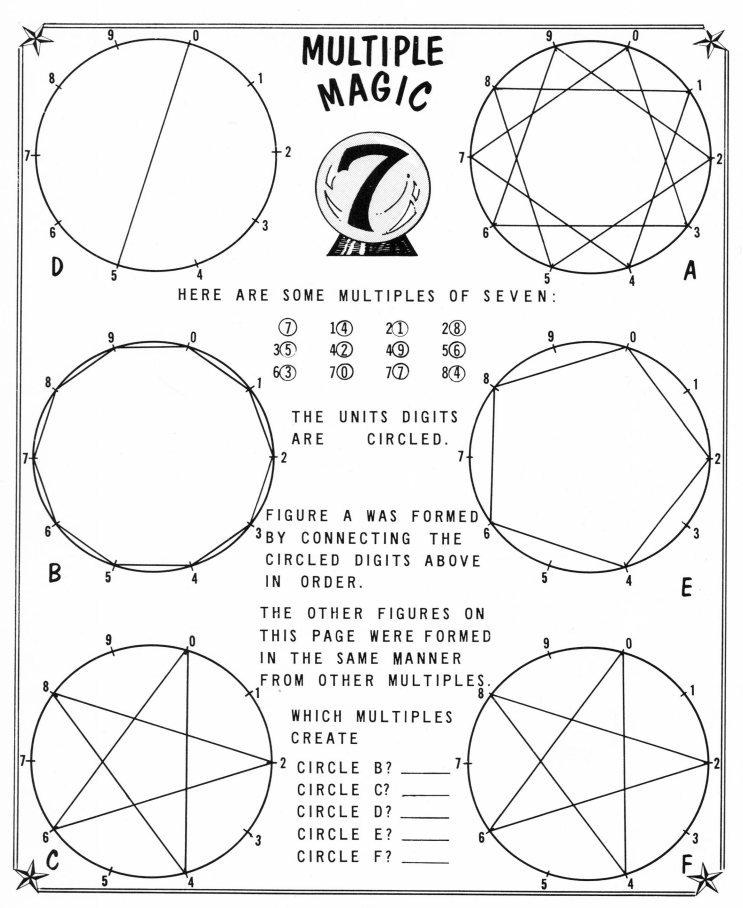

HERE ARE SOME MULTIPLES OF SEVEN:

⑦   1④   2①   2⑧
3⑤   4②   4⑨   5⑥
6③   7⓪   7⑦   8④

THE UNITS DIGITS ARE CIRCLED.

FIGURE A WAS FORMED BY CONNECTING THE CIRCLED DIGITS ABOVE IN ORDER.

THE OTHER FIGURES ON THIS PAGE WERE FORMED IN THE SAME MANNER FROM OTHER MULTIPLES.

WHICH MULTIPLES CREATE

CIRCLE B? _____
CIRCLE C? _____
CIRCLE D? _____
CIRCLE E? _____
CIRCLE F? _____

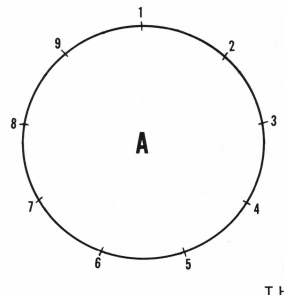

A

MULTIPLE MAGIC 7

LETS LOOK AT THE MULTIPLES OF 7 AGAIN.

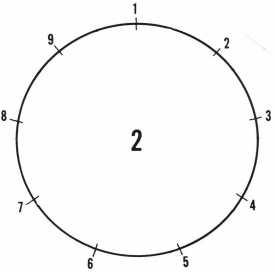

2

SUM THE DIGITS. IF THE SUM IS GREATER THAN 9, SUM THE DIGITS OF THE SUM.

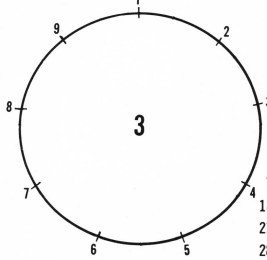

3

$7 \rightarrow \textcircled{7}$

$14 \rightarrow 1 + 4 = \textcircled{5}$

$21 \rightarrow 2 + 1 = \textcircled{3}$

$28 \rightarrow 2 + 8 = 10 \rightarrow 1 + 0 = \textcircled{1}$

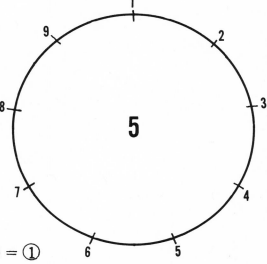

5

CONTINUE ON SCRATCH PAPER UNTIL YOU GET 7 AGAIN.

NEXT, CONNECT THE CIRCLED POINTS IN ORDER IN CIRCLE A. WHAT FIGURE DID YOU GET?

DO THE SAME EXERCISE USING THE MULTIPLES OF THE NUMBERS IN THE CIRCLES.

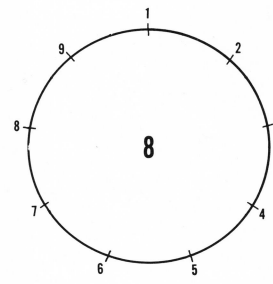

8

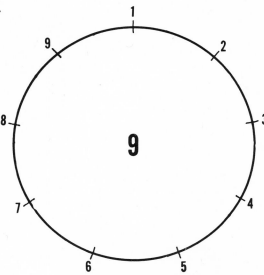

9

19

HIDDEN SHAPES

THE EIGHT SHADED FIGURES BELOW ARE ALL CREATED FROM THE PATTERN IN THE CENTER. CAN YOU SEE HOW EACH PATTERN WAS MADE? WHICH IS AN OPTICAL ILLUSION? PLACE A PIECE OF TRACING PAPER OVER THE CENTER PATTERN AND MAKE THESE DESIGNS OR SOME OF YOUR OWN CREATION.

COIN CAPERS

MOVE THE PENNY BETWEEN
THE NICKEL AND DIME WITHOUT
TOUCHING THE DIME OR MOVING
THE NICKEL.

IT CAN
BE DONE!

B.
GUESS HOW MANY
PENNIES IN A PILE IT
WILL TAKE TO EQUAL THE
HEIGHT OF A PENNY ON
EDGE. AFTER YOU HAVE
GUESSED, TRY IT AND SEE.

C.

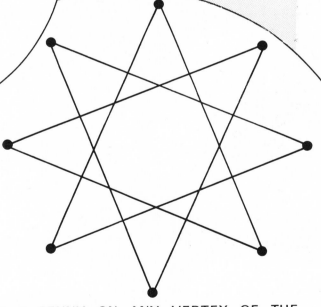

PLACE A PENNY ON ANY VERTEX OF THE
STAR AND SLIDE IT ALONG ONE LINE
TO ANOTHER OPEN VERTEX. CONTINUE
THE SAME WAY UNTIL YOU HAVE
PLACED SEVEN PENNIES ON
THE EIGHT VERTICES.

STRAW POLYHEDRA

CAN YOU MAKE THESE FIVE
REGULAR POLYHEDRA MODELS FROM
DRINKING STRAWS?

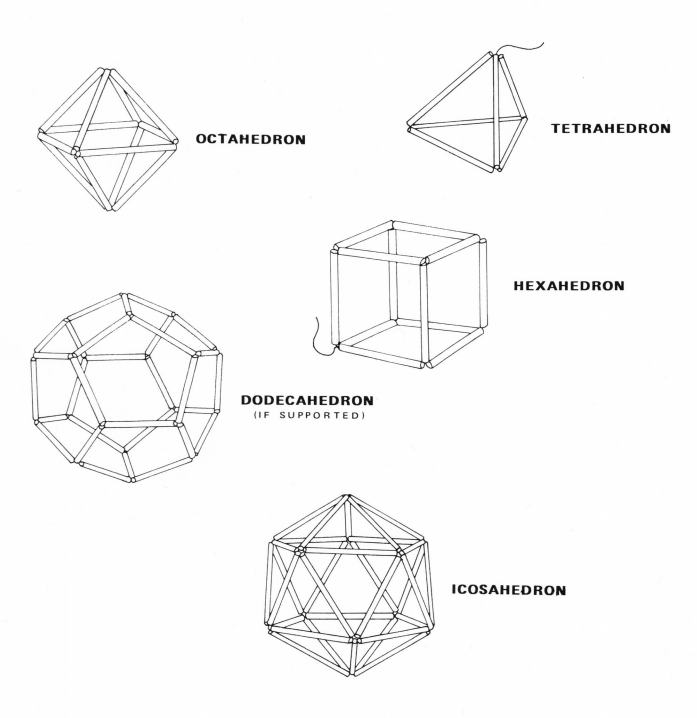

OCTAHEDRON

TETRAHEDRON

HEXAHEDRON

DODECAHEDRON
(IF SUPPORTED)

ICOSAHEDRON

A WHOLE THING

1. IF THE SHADED SECTION OF THE KITE REPRESENTS **ONE**, THEN:

1a. DOTTED REGION

_____

1b. CROSSED REGION

_____

1c. STRIPED REGION

_____

1d. WHITE REGION

_____

2. IF THE SHADED AREA IS 2:

2a. DOTTED REGION

_____

2b. CROSSED REGION

_____

2c. STRIPED REGION

_____

23

WHICH ONE DIFFERS ?

OPTICAL ILLUSIONS

ARE THE EIGHT CLOSED CURVES REALLY CIRCLES? WHICH DARK CIRCLE IN THE CENTER FIGURE IS 'BEHIND' THE OTHER THREE? ARE YOU LOOKING AT THE FOUR SHADED FIGURES FROM THE TOP?

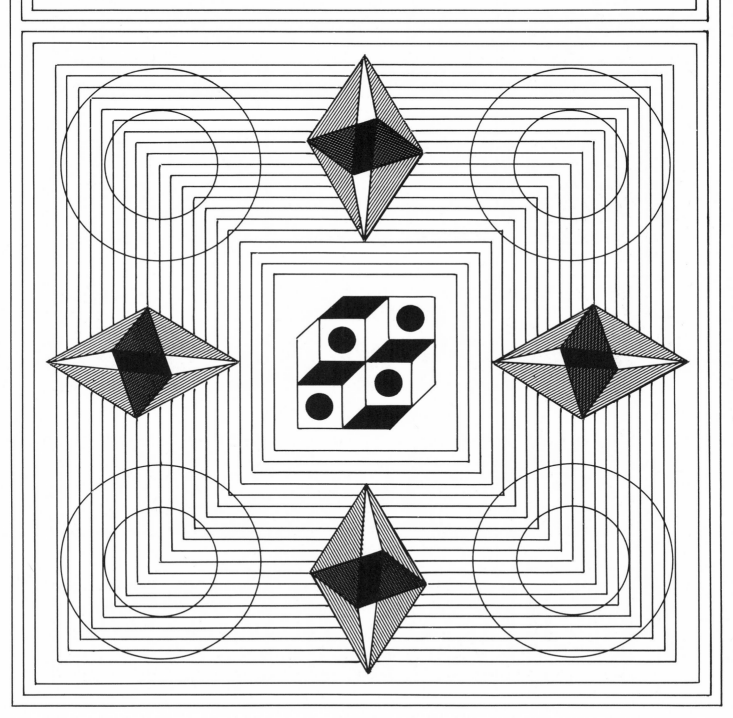

EQUATION PUZZLE

Solve these:

1) $2n = 14$ n = ____
2) $n + 8 = 18$ n = ____
3) $17 \times n = 51$ n = ____
4) $3 \times 3 \times 3 = n$ n = ____
5) $0 \times 58 = n$ n = ____
6) $25 \div n = 5$ n = ____
7) $7 \times 8 = n$ n = ____
8) $3^2 = n$ n = ____
9) $32 \div 8 = n$ n = ____
10) $3n + 5 = 23$ n = ____
11) $n - 12 = 17$ n = ____
12) $n = 2^3$ n = ____
13) $20 - n = 16$ n = ____
14) $22 - n = 11$ n = ____
15) $2 \times 4 \times 2 = n$ n = ____
16) $108 \div n = 12$ n = ____

Solve these:

17) $75 \div 15 = n$ n = ____
18) $1 \times 1 \times 1 = n$ n = ____
19) $4n = 28$ n = ____
20) $2 \times 2 \times 3 = n$ n = ____
21) $10^2 = n$ n = ____
22) $2 \times 7 \times 4 = n$ n = ____
23) $n + 2 = 31$ n = ____
24) $50 - n = 35$ n = ____
25) $35 \div 35 = n$ n = ____
26) $36 \div 3 = n$ n = ____
27) $n + n + n = 45$ n = ____
28) $n \div 4 = 9$ n = ____
29) $n \times n = 36$ n = ____
30) $0 \div 5 = n$ n = ____
31) $n \div 9 = 4$ n = ____
32) $3n - 2 = 22$ n = ____

5

9

16

4

.1

START
8

7   15
56   12

11   •100

27   •3

.0

36   6   10   29

SOLVE EACH EQUATION AND DRAW STRAIGHT LINES CONNECTING THE POINTS NAMED BY
THE SOLUTIONS. COMPLETE THE DESIGN BY CONNECTING THE LAST POINT TO THE FIRST.

26

HOW BIG IS TEN MILLION ?

A ONE DOLLAR BILL IS APPROXIMATELY 15 cm LONG. ABOUT HOW FAR WILL 10,000,000 ONE DOLLAR BILLS REACH IF LAID END TO END?

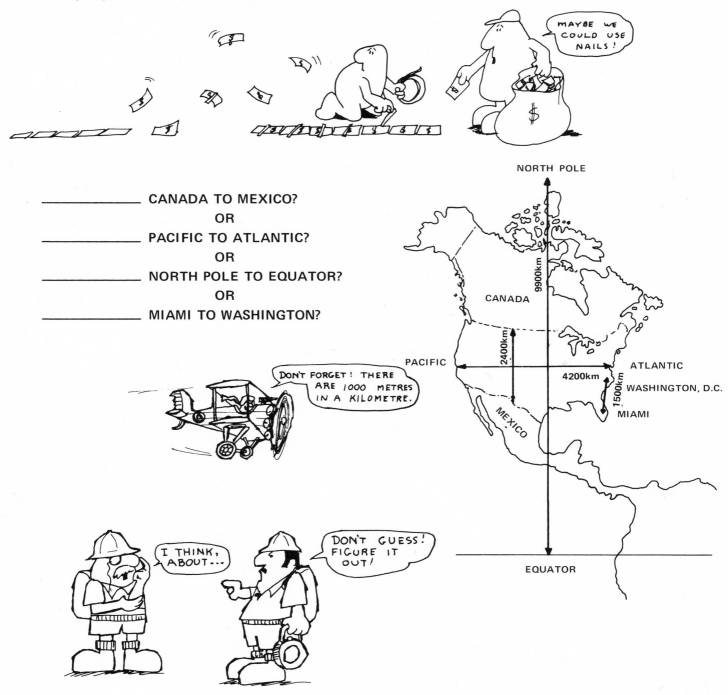

_____ CANADA TO MEXICO?
OR
_____ PACIFIC TO ATLANTIC?
OR
_____ NORTH POLE TO EQUATOR?
OR
_____ MIAMI TO WASHINGTON?

POLYHEDRA PUZZLE

CAN YOU PIECE TOGETHER
THE NINE SHAPES BELOW
TO FORM A STELLATED
DODECAHEDRON LIKE THE
ONE AT THE RIGHT?

28

FOUR CUBE PUZZLE

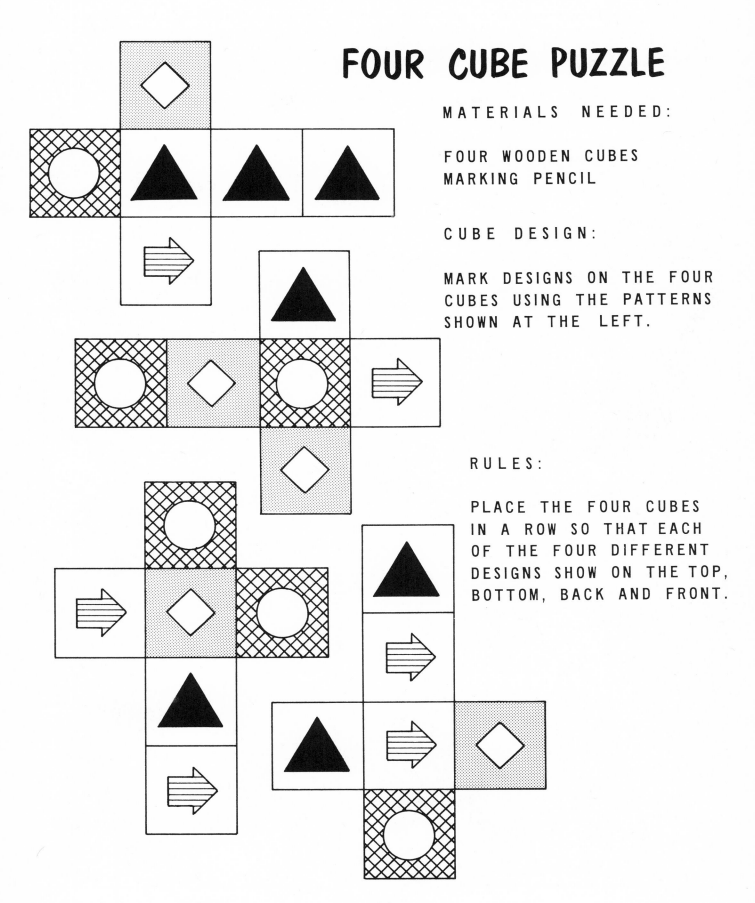

MATERIALS NEEDED:

FOUR WOODEN CUBES
MARKING PENCIL

CUBE DESIGN:

MARK DESIGNS ON THE FOUR
CUBES USING THE PATTERNS
SHOWN AT THE LEFT.

RULES:

PLACE THE FOUR CUBES
IN A ROW SO THAT EACH
OF THE FOUR DIFFERENT
DESIGNS SHOW ON THE TOP,
BOTTOM, BACK AND FRONT.

29

YOU START BY MAKING THREE ROWS OF TALLY MARKS, 3 MARKS IN ONE ROW, 5 MARKS IN ANOTHER, AND 7 MARKS IN THE LAST!

TWO PEOPLE PLAY AND TAKE TURNS ERASING MARKS. A PLAYER MAY ERASE AS MANY MARKS IN ONE ROW AS HE LIKES DURING HIS TURN.

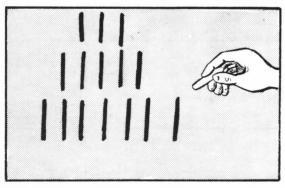

JEFF JUST ERASED THREE MARKS IN THE BOTTOM ROW. NOW IT IS BIFF'S TURN.

LOOK! BIFF HAS ERASED ALL OF THE MIDDLE ROW. YOU CAN ERASE ANY AMOUNT OF MARKS IN ANY ONE ROW!

JEFF IS ERASING ONE MARK IN THE BOTTOM ROW.

BIFF ERASES TWO MARKS IN THE TOP ROW.

OH, OH! I THINK BIFF HAS HAD IT!

MY TURN!

YEP! JEFF WON. HE LEFT BIFF WITH ONE MARK!

HEY! THAT LOOKS LIKE A GOOD GAME. LET'S PLAY!

OK! I GUESS THE GUYS ARE THROUGH!

NOTE: 3-5-7 IS THE KIND OF GAME WHERE YOU LEARN BY OBSERVING PATTERNS. IF YOU GET INTO A SITUATION AND LOSE, TRY TO AVOID THAT SITUATION NEXT TIME.

DO YOU THINK IT MATTERS WHO TAKES THE FIRST TURN?

SPAGHETTI MAZE

IN THE MAZE BELOW, FIND WHICH GATES ARE CONNECTED.

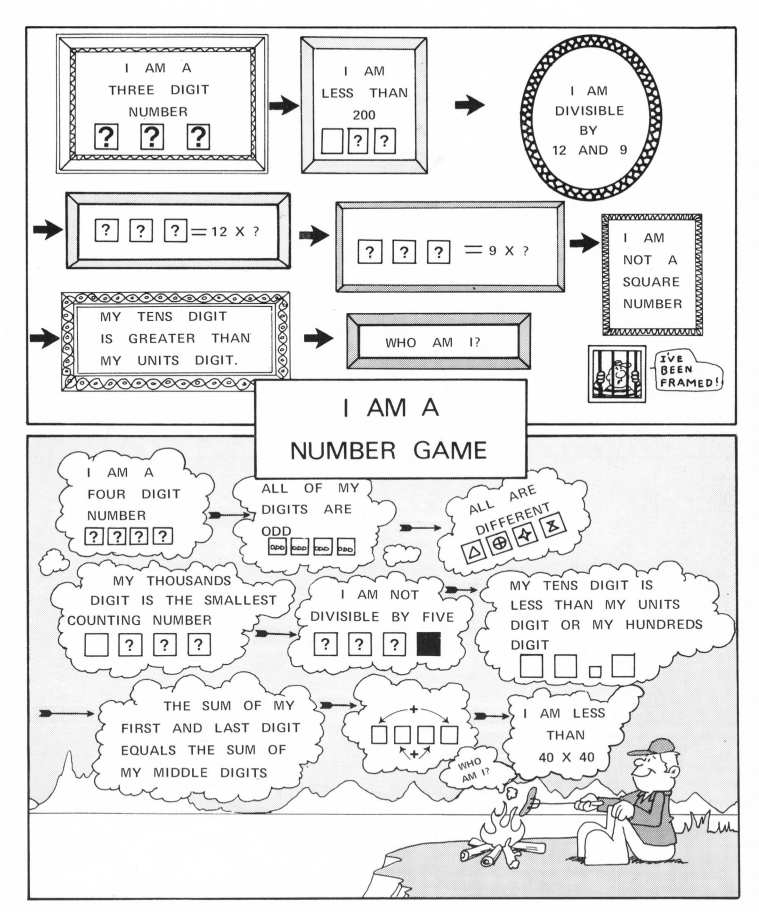

LINE DESIGN

CONNECT EACH POINT IN THE CIRCLE WITH BOTH POINTS THAT LIE THREE POINTS AWAY. THE INTERIOR POLYGON IS CALLED A **DODECAGON**. (12 SIDES)

CONNECT EACH POINT ON THE CIRCLE WITH EVERY POINT ON THE CIRCLE. USE A SHARP PENCIL OR A BALL POINT PEN. BE ACCURATE AND YOU WILL HAVE MADE AN ATTRACTIVE GEOMETRIC DESIGN.

PRIME FACTOR TENTS

FILL IN THE OPEN TRIANGLES

35

NUMBER PATTERNS

CAN YOU FIND A PATTERN IN THE ARRAY OF NUMBERS AT THE RIGHT? WHEN YOU FIND IT, COMPLETE THE FIGURE.

BUZZ-OFF!

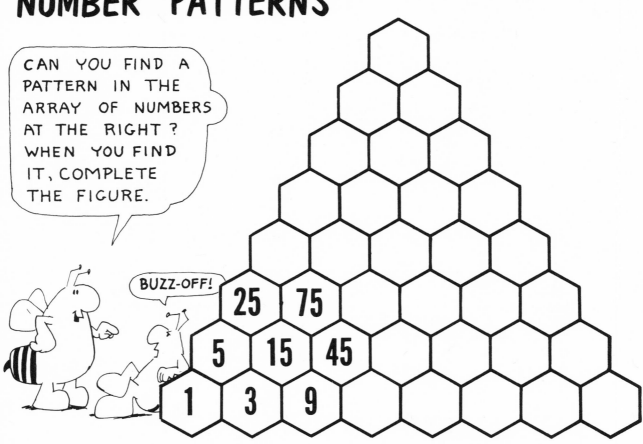

USING THE RULES IN THE PATTERN ABOVE, COMPLETE THE HEXAGONAL CELLS BELOW.

BEEHAVE!

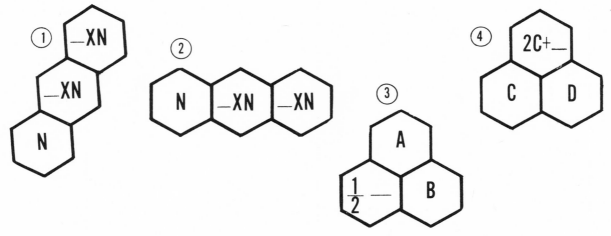

HOW MANY?

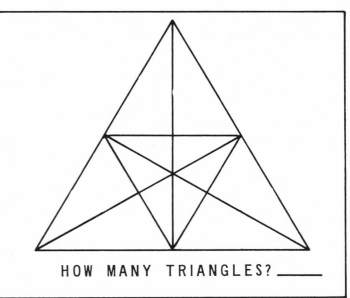

HOW MANY TRIANGLES? _____

29 26 10 7 5
15 4
1 2
27 21 16
19 23
8 9
12 28
11 17 24
35 202
6 14 18 3

HOW MANY PRIME NUMBERS? _____

HOW MANY SEGMENTS CONNECT
ALL PAIRS OF POINTS? _____

HOW MANY DIFFERENT
ANGLES LESS THAN 90? _____

TILE TRIAL

USE ANY **THREE** OF THESE TILES TO COMPLETE THE FOLLOWING:

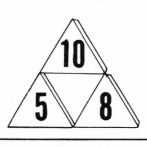

EXAMPLE:

$$40 \div 8 \times 5 = 25$$

USE (+, —, X, ÷)

1

 = 0

2

= 1

3

= 3

4

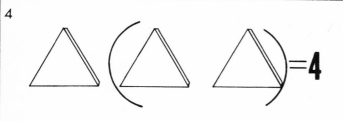 = 4

5

 = 7

6

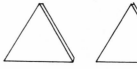 = 9

7

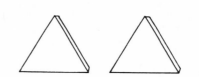 = 10

8

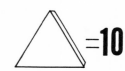 = 16

CAN YOU FORM ANY OTHER EQUATIONS, USING THREE OF THESE TILES THAT EQUAL LESS THAN 25?

AREA AND PERIMETER

ON THE GRID LINES BELOW DRAW EIGHT DIFFERENT RECTANGLES WITH A PERIMETER OF 72 UNITS. ALL LINES MUST BE ON THESE GRIDS.

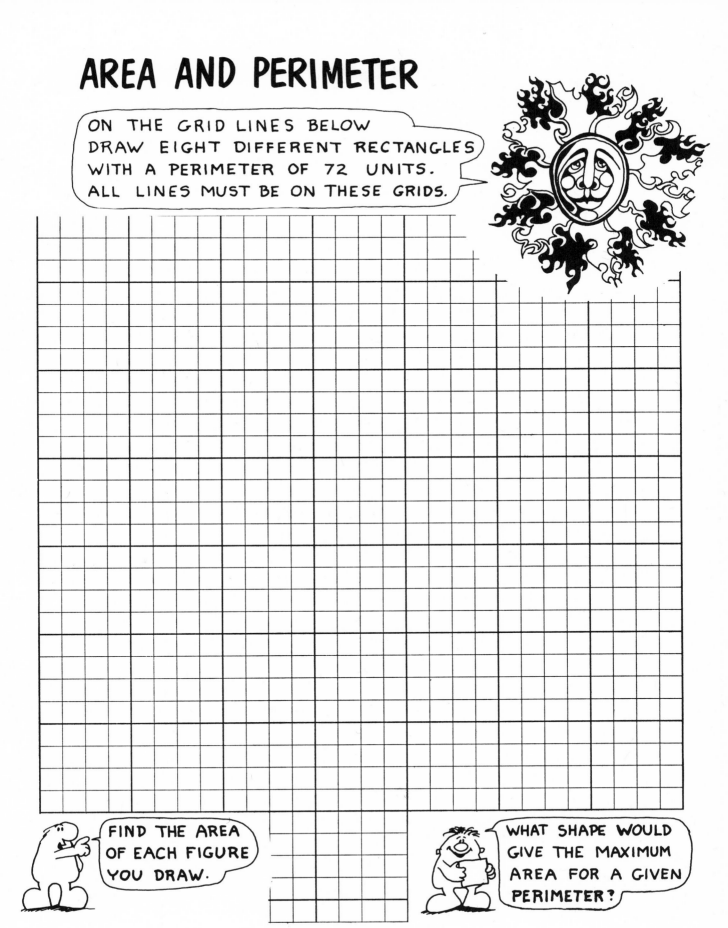

FIND THE AREA OF EACH FIGURE YOU DRAW.

WHAT SHAPE WOULD GIVE THE MAXIMUM AREA FOR A GIVEN PERIMETER?

GIVING DIRECTIONS

GIVE DIRECTIONS FROM A TO B, B TO C,
C TO D, D TO A, E TO B, AND F TO C.
WATCH THE ONE—WAY STREETS!

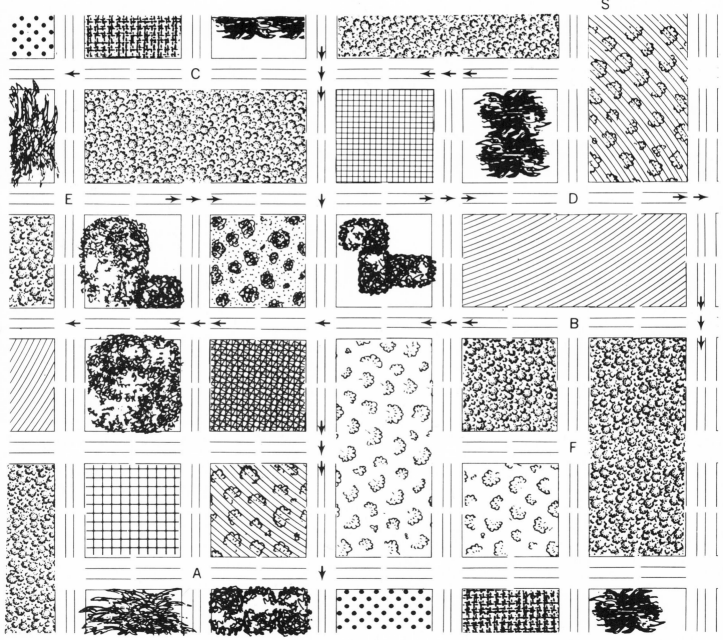

PROBABILITY

... IS A FUN <u>BRANCH</u> OF MATHEMATICS.

... IS THE STUDY OF CHANCE

... STARTED WITH A QUARREL BETWEEN TWO 17th CENTURY FRENCHMEN.

WHEN I TOSS TWO COINS IN THE AIR, **THREE** THINGS CAN HAPPEN.

I THINK **FOUR** THINGS CAN HAPPEN.

I SAY **THREE**!

I SAY **FOUR**!

THREE!

FOUR!

THREE!

FOUR!

SOMEBODY'S GOING TO FLIP!

A COIN EITHER COMES UP 2 HEADS, 2 TAILS, OR 1 HEAD AND 1 TAIL, AND THEIR CHANCES OF HAPPENING ARE THE SAME.

NO! A COIN EITHER COMES UP 2 HEADS, 2 TAILS, 1 HEAD AND 1 TAIL, OR 1 TAIL AND 1 HEAD, AND THE CHANCES OF THESE FOUR THINGS HAPPENING ARE THE SAME.

(CONTINUED)

41

LET'S SEE WHICH SIDE **YOU** WOULD TAKE. BUT FIRST DO THIS **EXPERIMENT**.

CALL ONE SIDE OF EACH COIN HEADS, THE OTHER, TAILS.

HEADS   TAILS

YOU NEED TWO COINS.

TOSS THE TWO COINS 100 TIMES.

IF THE COINS LAND LIKE THIS...

...MAKE A MARK UNDER **TWO HEADS**.

IF THE COINS LAND LIKE THIS...

...MAKE A MARK UNDER **TWO TAILS**.

IF THE COINS LAND LIKE THIS...

...OR THIS

MAKE A MARK UNDER **ONE HEAD—ONE TAIL**.

USE THIS CHART.

TWO HEADS	TWO TAILS	ONE HEAD ONE TAIL

AFTER 100 TOSSES DID EACH OF THESE THREE OUTCOMES HAPPEN ABOUT THE SAME NUMBER OF TIMES?

(CONTINUED)

PROBABILITY

DID YOU FIND THAT ONE HEAD AND ONE TAIL HAPPENS ABOUT **TWICE** AS OFTEN AS TWO HEADS OR TWO TAILS?

I'M STILL TOSSING.

PROBABILITY TELLS US WHAT IS **LIKELY** TO HAPPEN, NOT WHAT WILL HAPPEN.

IT IS **PROBABLE** THAT:

TWO HEADS COME UP ABOUT ¼ OF THE TIME.

TWO TAILS COME UP ABOUT ¼ OF THE TIME.

ONE HEAD AND ONE TAIL COME UP ABOUT ½ OF THE TIME.

2 HEADS	2 TAILS	1 HEAD 1 TAIL
꘡꘡꘡꘡ ꘡꘡꘡꘡	꘡꘡꘡꘡ ꘡꘡꘡꘡	꘡꘡꘡꘡ ꘡꘡꘡꘡
꘡꘡꘡꘡ ꘡꘡꘡꘡	꘡꘡꘡꘡ ꘡꘡꘡꘡	꘡꘡꘡꘡ ꘡꘡꘡꘡
꘡꘡꘡꘡	꘡꘡꘡꘡	꘡꘡꘡꘡ ꘡꘡꘡꘡
		꘡꘡꘡꘡ ꘡꘡꘡꘡
		꘡꘡꘡꘡ ꘡꘡꘡꘡

COULD THE TWO COINS HAVE LANDED BOTH TAILS EVERY ONE OF THE 100 TRIALS?

YES, BUT IT'S NOT VERY **PROBABLE**.

DID YOUR CLASSMATES COME UP WITH ABOUT THE SAME CHART AS YOU DID?

(CONTINUED)

43

PROBABILITY

TRY THIS EXPERIMENT WITH A PENNY AND A NICKEL.

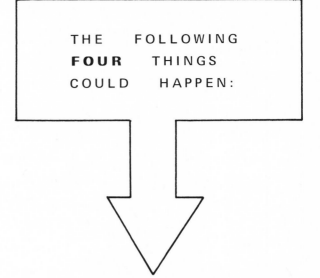

THE FOLLOWING **FOUR** THINGS COULD HAPPEN:

PENNY HEADS NICKEL HEADS	PENNY TAILS NICKEL TAILS	PENNY HEADS NICKEL TAILS	PENNY TAILS NICKEL HEADS

YOU **PROBABLY** WILL HAVE EACH OF THE FOUR **EVENTS** ABOVE HAPPEN **ABOUT** AN EQUAL NUMBER OF TIMES.

DON'T USE A TWO-HEADED COIN.

(CONTINUED)

PROBABILITIES

ARE USUALLY STATED AS FRACTIONS.

WHEN TOSSING TWO COINS, THE PROBABILITIES OF BOTH COINS LANDING HEADS IS **ONE-FOURTH**.

$\frac{1}{4}$

WHEN TOSSING TWO COINS, THE PROBABILITY OF BOTH COINS LANDING TAILS IS **ONE-FOURTH**.

$\frac{1}{4}$

WHEN TOSSING TWO COINS, THE PROBABILITY OF ONE HEAD AND ONE TAIL IS **ONE-HALF**.

$\frac{1}{2}$

$\frac{1}{4} + \frac{1}{4} + \frac{1}{2} = 1$

THE SUM OF THE PROBABILITIES OF ALL THINGS THAT COULD HAPPEN IS **ALWAYS ONE**.

TRY AN EXPERIMENT WITH 3 COINS.

TINKERTOTALS

PLACE THE NUMBERS
1, 2, 3, 4, 5
IN THE CIRCLES AT
THE RIGHT SO THAT
FOUR CIRCLES IN A ROW
TOTAL 24.

PLACE THE
NUMBERS 3, 7, 9, 10, 11, 12 IN
THE CIRCLES AT THE LEFT
SO THAT FOUR CIRCLES IN
A ROW TOTAL
26.

PLACE THE NUMBERS
8, 9, 10, 11, 12, 13, 14 IN
THE CIRCLES AT THE
RIGHT SO THAT FOUR
CIRCLES IN A ROW TOTAL
30.

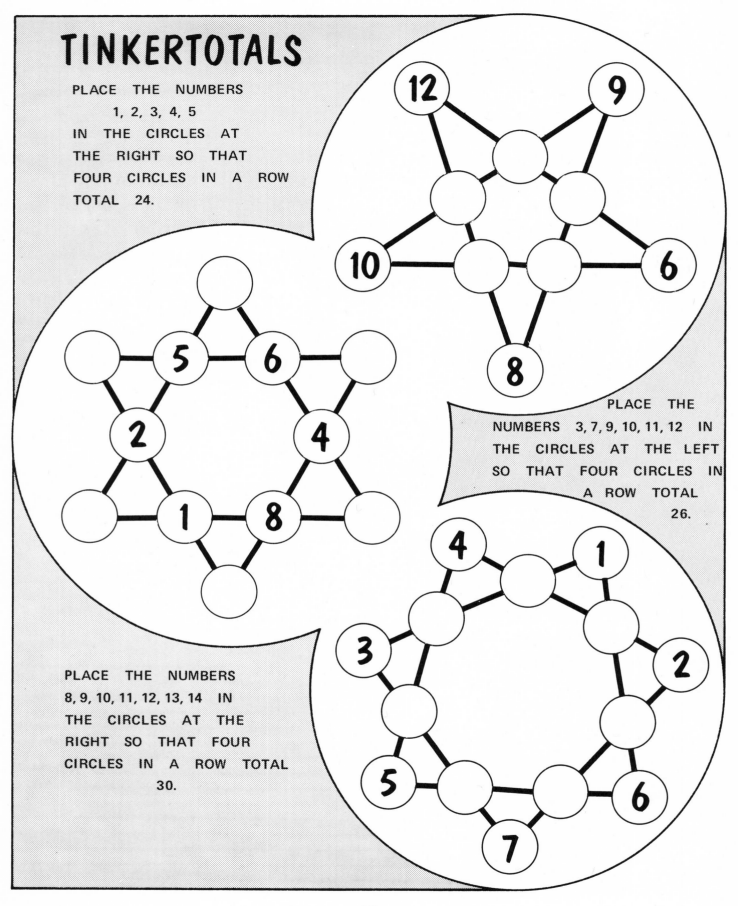

46

FIND MY PATTERN.

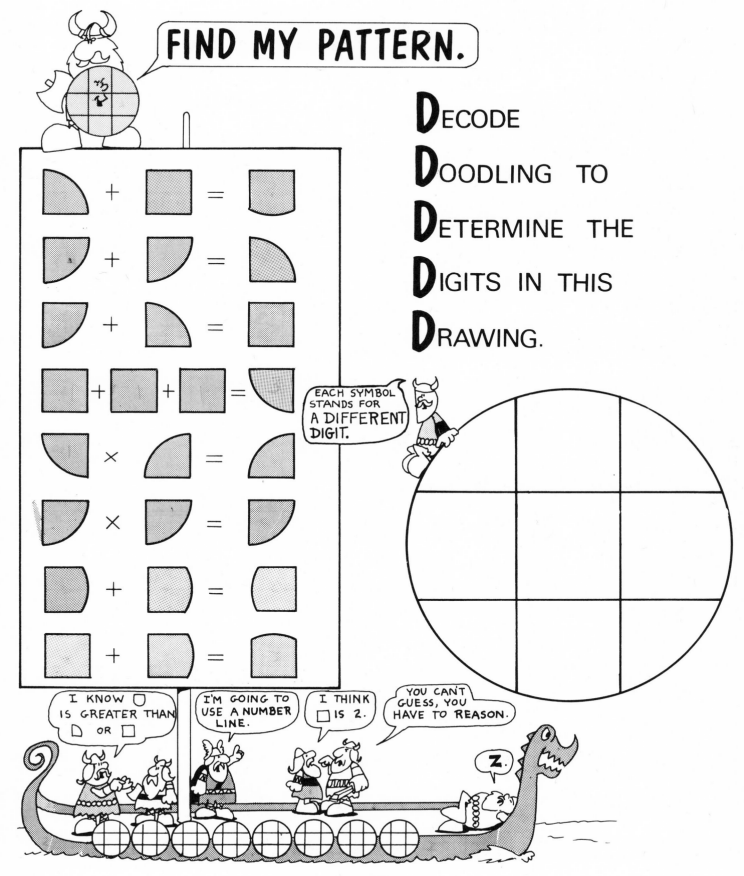

DECODE
DOODLING TO
DETERMINE THE
DIGITS IN THIS
DRAWING.

EACH SYMBOL STANDS FOR A DIFFERENT DIGIT.

I KNOW ☐ IS GREATER THAN ☐ OR ☐

I'M GOING TO USE A NUMBER LINE.

I THINK ☐ IS 2.

YOU CAN'T GUESS, YOU HAVE TO REASON.

Z.

TRELLIS TWISTER

THE TRELLIS IN THE TOP LEFT-HAND CORNER IS ONE OF
THE OTHER EIGHT AS SEEN FROM THE BACK SIDE. WHICH ONE?

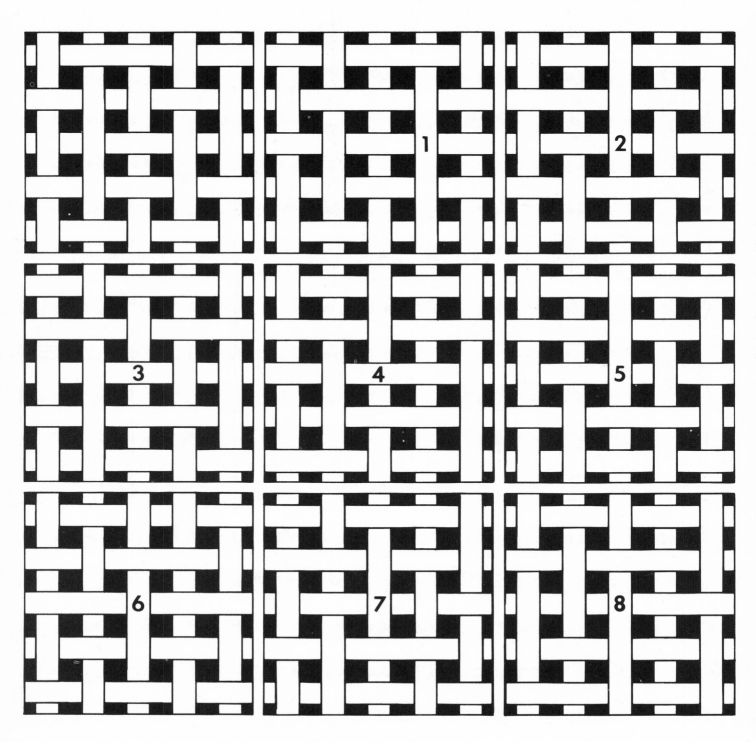

PROPORTIONAL DRAWING

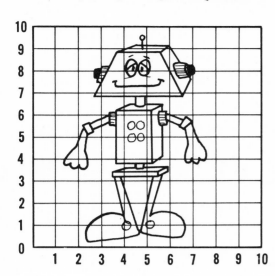

MAKE AN ENLARGEMENT OF THE DRAWING AT THE LEFT ON THE GRID BELOW.

A LINE ON THE SMALL GRID SHOULD BE LOCATED ON A CORRESPONDING POSITION ON THE LARGE GRID.

THE RATIO OF THE SEGMENTS IN THE SMALL DRAWING TO THE SEGMENTS IN THE LARGE DRAWING IS 2 TO 1.

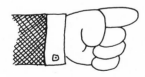

THE AREAS HAVE A RATIO OF 4 TO 1.

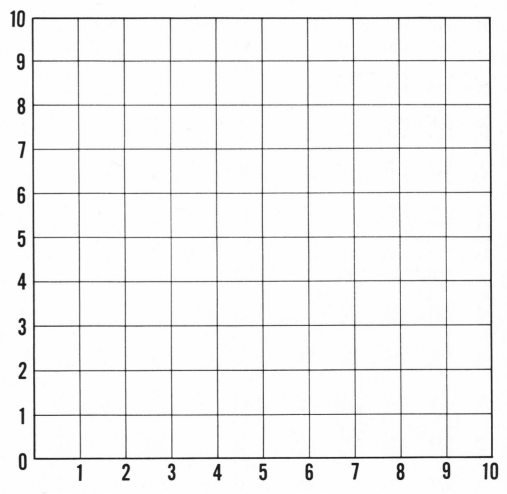

FIND THE AREA OF EACH CONSTELLATION ABOVE.

ONE SQUARE UNIT.

LOGIC LURE

FOX, DUCK, AND A BAG OF CORN

A MAN OWNED A FOX, A DUCK, AND A BAG OF CORN. ONE DAY HE WAS ON THE BANK OF A RIVER, WHERE THERE WAS A BOAT ONLY LARGE ENOUGH FOR HIM TO CROSS WITH ONE OF HIS POSSESSIONS. IF HE LEFT THE FOX AND DUCK ALONE, THE FOX WOULD EAT THE DUCK. IF HE LEFT THE DUCK AND THE CORN ALONE, THE DUCK WOULD EAT THE CORN. HOW DID HE GET SAFELY ACROSS THE RIVER WITH ALL THREE OF HIS POSSESSIONS?

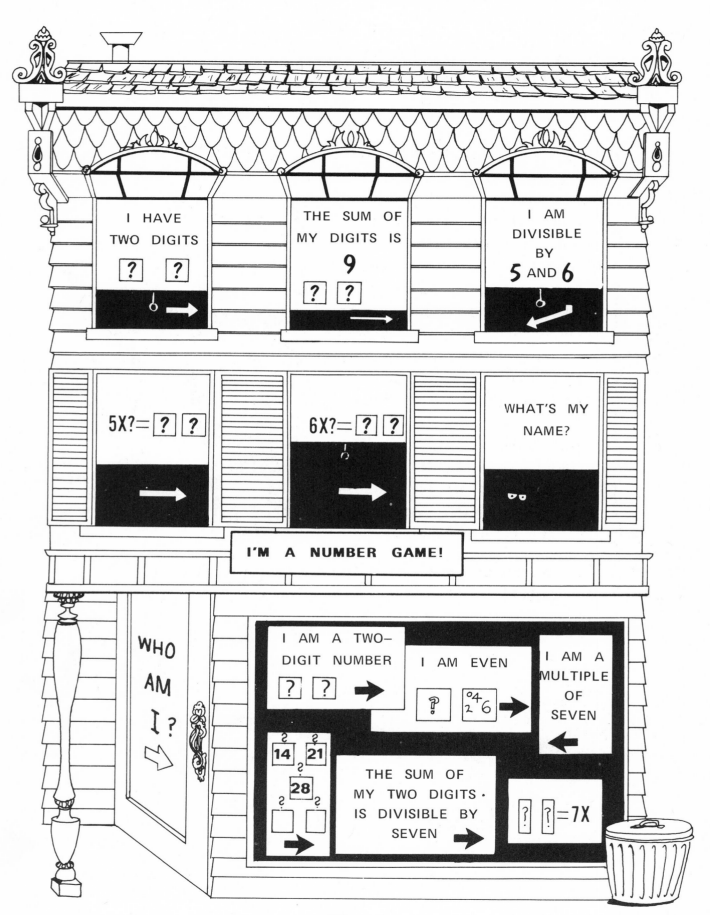

52

PENTAGONAL ARITHMETIC

HERE IS A FIVE-NUMBER ARITHMETIC SYSTEM. COUNT **COUNTER**CLOCKWISE AROUND THE PENTAGON. CAN YOU SEE THE PATTERNS IN THE "+" AND "x" TABLES BELOW AND COMPLETE THE TABLE?

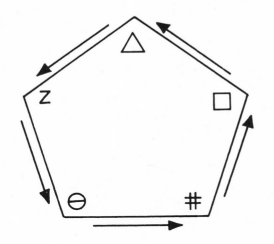

"+"	△	z	⊖	#	□
△					
z		⊖			
⊖		#			
#					
□					

WHAT SYMBOL ACTS LIKE ZERO?

WHAT SYMBOL ACTS LIKE ONE?

"x"	△	z	⊖	#	□
△					
z					□
⊖			□		
#					
□					

NILE TILE

EGYPTIAN TILES WOULD LOOK LIKE THIS:

EXAMPLE:

$$\frac{5}{12} = \boxed{} + \boxed{}$$

$\sqsubset = \frac{1}{2}$ $\oplus = \frac{2}{3}$

$\bigcirc = \frac{1}{3}$ $\bigcirc = \frac{1}{6}$ $\bigcirc = \frac{1}{4}$

1) $\frac{5}{6} = \boxed{} + \boxed{}$

2) $\frac{1}{2} = \boxed{} - \boxed{}$

3) $\frac{2}{3} = \boxed{} + \boxed{}$

4) $\frac{7}{12} = \boxed{} + \boxed{}$

5) $\frac{3}{4} = \boxed{} + \boxed{}$

6) $\frac{5}{12} = \boxed{} - \boxed{}$

7) $\frac{3}{4} = \boxed{} + \boxed{} + \boxed{}$

8) $\frac{7}{12} = \boxed{} + \boxed{} - \boxed{}$

54

FIBONACCI SEQUENCE MAZE

IN THE EARLY 13th CENTURY, AN ITALIAN BOY NAMED **FIBONACCI** HAD GREAT FUN MAKING UP NUMBER SERIES AND SEQUENCES. ONE OF THESE SEQUENCES IS NAMED AFTER HIM. THE **FIBONACCI SEQUENCE** IS FOUND IN THE STUDY OF GENETICS AND MANY PLACES IN NATURE.

IN THIS MAZE THERE ARE **TWO PATHS** USING THE FIBONACCI SEQUENCE FROM **1–987**.

ONE ON BLACK

ONE ON WHITE

FIND THEM BOTH.

1	1	2	4	7	5	8	6	144	7
1	1	11	3	10	5	9	13	8	89
5	2	17	13	5	15	21	88	55	14
12	12	3	33	16	8	55	34	143	233
9	5	34	14	21	34	13	89	144	234
55	67	8	17	21	21	35	89	144	178
68	7	65	13	22	376	34	233	233	232
9	108	377	43	301	55	377	377	609	34
173	610	304	377	89	378	233	610	610	999
987	201	34	105	87	144	611	378	987	987

FIBONACCI SEQUENCE

1 , 1 , 2 , 3 , 5 , 8 , ...

Multiply 5.4 by 10.
Multiply 4.7 by 100.
Multiply 73 by 100.
Multiply 31.4 by 10.
Multiply 876 by 100.
Multiply 47.3 by 100.
Multiply 51.34 by 10.
Multiply 4.78 by 1000.
Multiply 63.817 by 100.
Multiply 814 by 100.

Multiply 43.75 by 35.

OPERATION.

$$
\begin{array}{r}
43.75 \\
35 \\
\hline
218.75 \\
1312.5 \\
\hline
\text{Ans. } 1531.25
\end{array}
$$

Multiply 456 by 50.
Multiply 217 by 40.
Multiply 8.46 by 2100.
Multiply 1217 by 80.
Multiply 3468 by 230.

Multiply 765 by 203.

OPERATION.

$$
\begin{array}{r}
765 \\
203 \\
\hline
2295 \\
1530 \\
\hline
\text{Ans. } 155295
\end{array}
$$

Multiply 806 by 305.
Multiply 204 by 21.
Multiply 7060 by 40.
Multiply 8764 by 80.
Multiply 632.14 by 701.
Multiply 8007 by 102.
Multiply 654.32 by 47.
Multiply 300.07 by 903.
Multiply 634.16 by 80.
Multiply 718.9 by 70.
Multiply 876.12 by 700.
Multiply 652.1 by 35.
Multiply 817 by 80.
Multiply 9230 by 70.
Multiply 6724 by 45.
Multiply 18407 by 32.
Multiply 765.8 by 40.
Multiply 987.5 by 25.
Multiply 2040 by 75.
Multiply 6005 by 302.

$$7 \times 3 = 21$$
$$9 \times 8 = 72$$

Ye olde math

56

5×9? 11×6? 9×7? 5×5? 7×7? 8×11? 12×3? 10×4? 7×3? 5×3?

19. How many are 6×11? 10×6? 9×8? 5×10? 8×8? 4×11? 8×6? 9×3? 5×11? 2×9? 8×5? 12×2? 3×8?

20. How many are 7×5? 8×7? 12×6? 6×12? 10×9? 9×9? 5×6? 12×5? 6×7? 11×7? 11×3? 7×11? 3×6?

42. **Multiplication** is the process of finding how many units there are in any number of times a given number.

43. The **Multiplicand** is the number to be repeated.

The **Multiplier** is the number which shows how many times the multiplicand is to be taken.

The **Product** is the *result* of the multiplication.

The *Multiplicand* and *Multiplier* are called **Factors.**

44. The *sign of multiplication*, $\times$, signifies that the two numbers between which it stands are to be multiplied together; thus, $6 \times 5 = 30$, that is, six multiplied by five equals thirty; or, six times five are thirty.

45. *The multiplier is always an abstract number.*

The product is of the same kind as the multiplicand.

Thus, in Ex. 1, the multiplier is 3, not 3 oranges. We cannot take 4 cents 3 *oranges* times; but we take 4 cents 3 times, that is, as many times as there are units in the number of oranges, and the answer is *cents*, 3 times 4 cents $= 12$ cents.

PUZZLERS

HOW CAN THESE SIX SECTIONS OF CHAIN, EACH CONTAINING FOUR LINKS, BE JOINED INTO ONE CHAIN ... CUTTING LESS THAN FIVE LINKS?

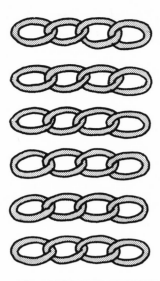

DRAW FOUR STRAIGHT LINES SO AS TO CROSS OUT EVERY DOT. DON'T CROSS A DOT MORE THAN ONCE.
DON'T RETRACE A LINE. DON'T LIFT THE PENCIL FROM THE PAPER UNTIL ALL NINE DOTS DOTS HAVE BEEN CROSSED.

SURE ARE A LOT OF DON'ts!

WHAT ONE NUMBER, WHICH ADDED SEPARATELY TO 100 AND 164, WILL MAKE THEM BOTH PERFECT SQUARE NUMBERS?

100
+
‾‾‾
☐

164
+
‾‾‾
☐

TRANSYLVANIA TRANSITIVITY

WHAT'S GOING ON HERE?

ITS A POLICE LINE UP!

ORDER IN THE COURT!

WHAT IS THE TRANSITIVE PROPERTY?

ED IS TALLER THAN NED. NED IS TALLER THAN RED. RED IS TALLER THAN TED. AL IS TALLER THAN RED, BUT SHORTER THAN NED. IKE IS STANDING BETWEEN SAL AND TODD, WHO IS SHORTER THAN ED, BUT TALLER THAN IKE. VAN IS STANDING BETWEEN ED AND IAN, WHO IS STANDING NEXT TO TODD. THERE ARE SEVEN MEN STANDING BETWEEN VAN AND TED.

CAN YOU FILL IN THE NAMES OF THESE SUSPECTS?

ITS EASIER IF YOU TEAR OUT TEN SLIPS OF PAPER.

HERE ARE SOME MORE LOGIC TESTS LIKE THE ONES IN AFTERMATH I AND II. A CHANGES TO B LIKE C CHANGES TO WHAT NUMBERS?

CIRCLE ONE OF THE FIVE CHOICES.

	A	B	C	1	2	3	4	5
1								
2								
3								
4								
5								
6								
7								

WHICH ONE DIFFERS ?

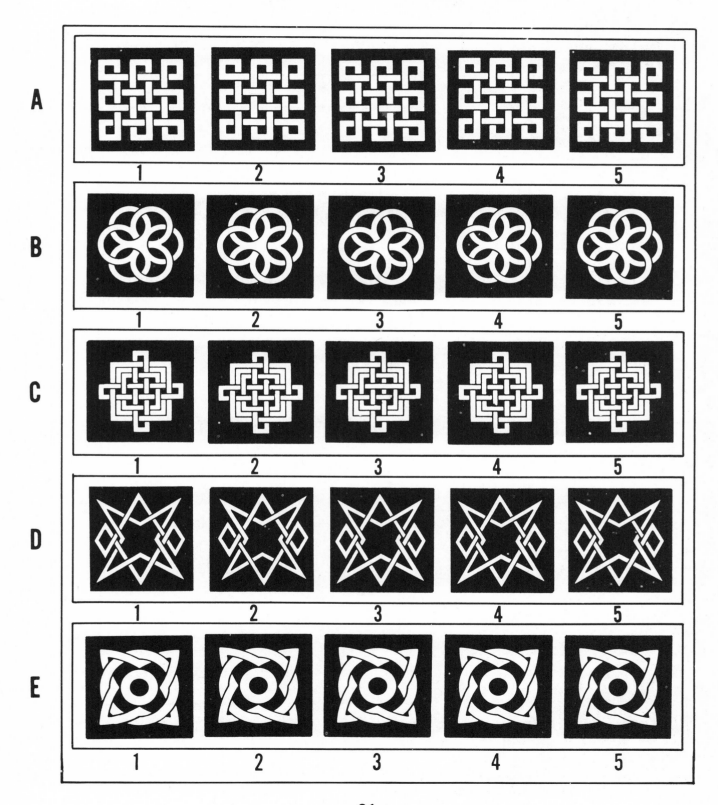

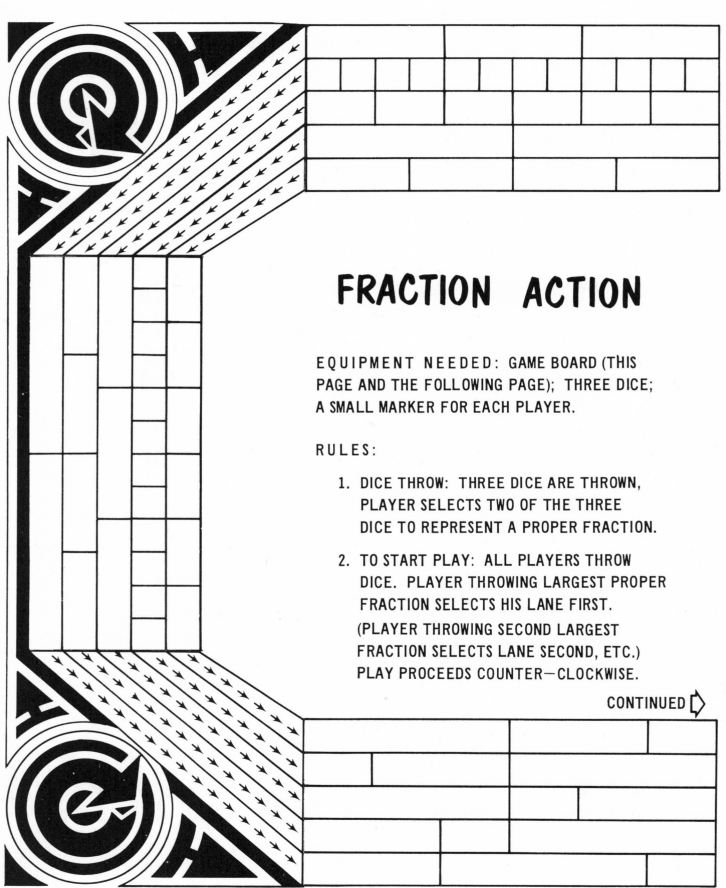

FRACTION ACTION

EQUIPMENT NEEDED: GAME BOARD (THIS PAGE AND THE FOLLOWING PAGE); THREE DICE; A SMALL MARKER FOR EACH PLAYER.

RULES:

1. DICE THROW: THREE DICE ARE THROWN, PLAYER SELECTS TWO OF THE THREE DICE TO REPRESENT A PROPER FRACTION.

2. TO START PLAY: ALL PLAYERS THROW DICE. PLAYER THROWING LARGEST PROPER FRACTION SELECTS HIS LANE FIRST. (PLAYER THROWING SECOND LARGEST FRACTION SELECTS LANE SECOND, ETC.) PLAY PROCEEDS COUNTER—CLOCKWISE.

CONTINUED ▷

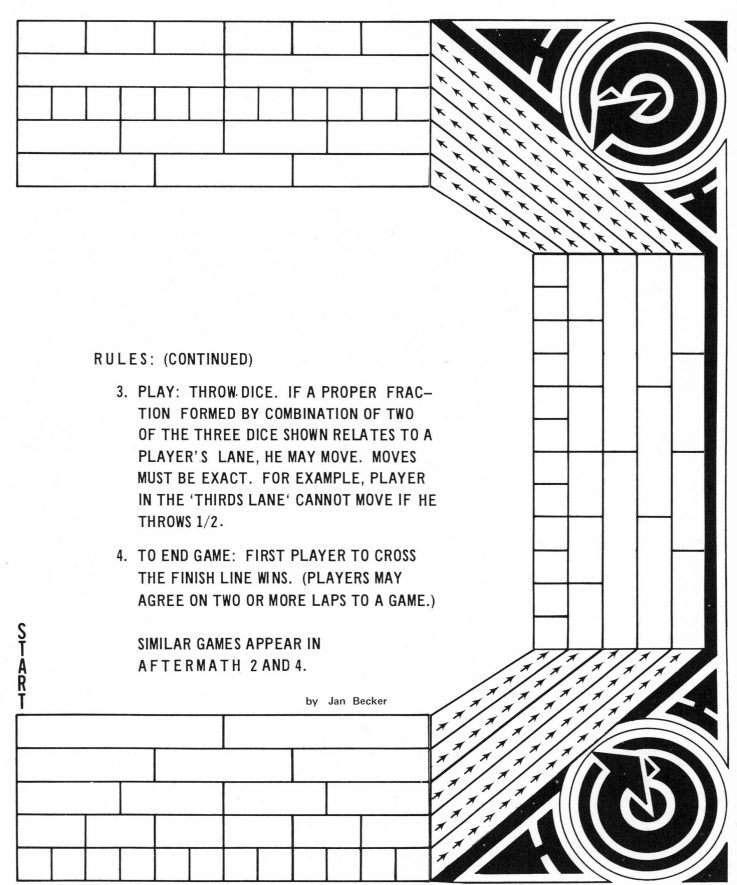

RULES: (CONTINUED)

3. PLAY: THROW DICE. IF A PROPER FRAC-
TION FORMED BY COMBINATION OF TWO
OF THE THREE DICE SHOWN RELATES TO A
PLAYER'S LANE, HE MAY MOVE. MOVES
MUST BE EXACT. FOR EXAMPLE, PLAYER
IN THE 'THIRDS LANE' CANNOT MOVE IF HE
THROWS 1/2.

4. TO END GAME: FIRST PLAYER TO CROSS
THE FINISH LINE WINS. (PLAYERS MAY
AGREE ON TWO OR MORE LAPS TO A GAME.)

SIMILAR GAMES APPEAR IN
AFTERMATH 2 AND 4.

by Jan Becker

START

WHAT'S MY WORD?

IN THESE PROBLEMS, LETTERS HAVE REPLACED NUMBERS. BY STUDYING THE PROBLEMS CAN YOU FIND THE **CODE WORD**?

```
  0 1 2 3 4 5 6 7 8 9
```

```
  FACE
+  NO
------
 FANS
```

```
  OFF
-  ON
------
  ONO
```

```
        ROLL
    F ) EARN
        E
        ---
         A
         F
        ---
         RR
         RC
        ---
         RN
         RC
        ---
          N
```

```
  OR
×  OR
------
  OFF
```

```
  AREA
- LAKE
------
   ACE
```

$$00 \times 00 = ORO$$

$$AR \times OC = ARC$$

```
  FARE
- FOOL
------
   LON
```

$$LA \div K = E$$

64

SHOWN BELOW ARE SOME OF THE SHAPES THAT CAN BE MADE FROM ONE, TWO, THREE OR FOUR SQUARES JOINED ON AN EDGE. CAN YOU FIT THEM IN THE 5X5 SQUARE?

IT'S OKAY TO TURN OR FLIP THE SHAPES.

THIS IS ONE OF TWELVE SHAPES THAT CAN BE MADE FROM FIVE SQUARES. USE IT WITH THE EIGHT PIECES ABOVE TO COMPLETE THE 5 X 6 RECTANGLE.

CAN YOU FIND THE OTHER ELEVEN FIVE—SQUARE SHAPES?

WILL EACH OF THE ELEVEN MAKE A 5 X 6 RECTANGLE WITH THE EIGHT PIECES ABOVE?

PRIME MAZE

THERE ARE 32 SPIRALING PATHS OF SQUARES TO THE CENTER IN THE FIGURE BELOW. ONLY ONE OF THESE IS COMPLETELY MADE OF PRIME NUMBERS. CAN YOU FIND THE PRIME PATH?

CODE MODE

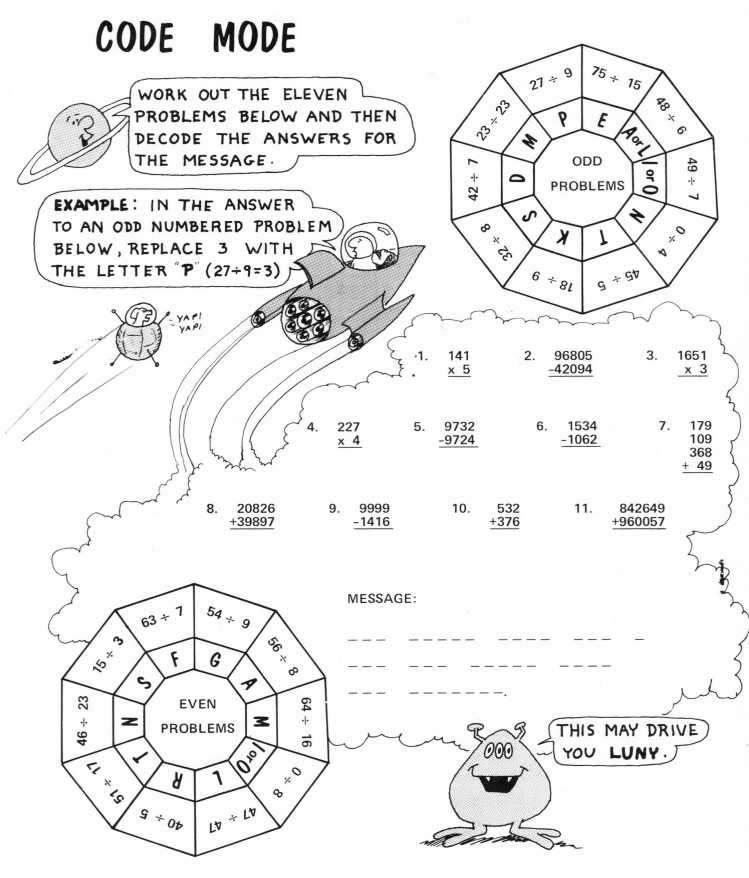

WORK OUT THE ELEVEN PROBLEMS BELOW AND THEN DECODE THE ANSWERS FOR THE MESSAGE.

EXAMPLE: IN THE ANSWER TO AN ODD NUMBERED PROBLEM BELOW, REPLACE 3 WITH THE LETTER "P" (27÷9=3)

YAP! YAP!

ODD PROBLEMS

27 ÷ 9 | 75 ÷ 15 | 48 ÷ 6 | 49 ÷ 7 | 0 ÷ 4 | 45 ÷ 5 | 18 ÷ 9 | 32 ÷ 8 | 42 ÷ 7 | 23 ÷ 23

P E A or L/ or 0 N T K S D M

1.　141
　　x 5

2.　96805
　　−42094

3.　1651
　　x 3

4.　227
　　x 4

5.　9732
　　−9724

6.　1534
　　−1062

7.　179
　　109
　　368
　　+ 49

8.　20826
　　+39897

9.　9999
　　−1416

10.　532
　　+376

11.　842649
　　+960057

MESSAGE:

_ _ _　_ _ _ _ _　_ _ _ _　_ _ _　_

_ _ _　_ _ _　_ _ _ _　_ _ _ _

_ _ _　_ _ _ _ _ _ _.

EVEN PROBLEMS

63 ÷ 7 | 54 ÷ 9 | 56 ÷ 8 | 64 ÷ 16 | 0 ÷ 8 | 47 ÷ 47 | 40 ÷ 5 | 51 ÷ 17 | 46 ÷ 23 | 15 ÷ 3

S F G A M I or 0 L R T N

THIS MAY DRIVE YOU **LUNY.**

67

CREATIVE COLORING

69

PLOTTING POINTS

DO YOU REMEMBER HOW TO PLOT POINTS ON A GRID?

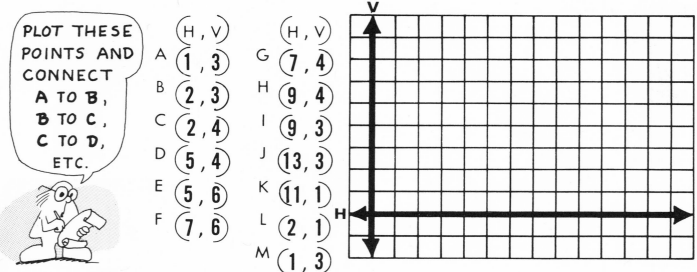

PLOT THESE POINTS AND CONNECT A TO B, B TO C, C TO D, ETC.

	(H , V)		(H , V)
A	(1 , 3)	G	(7 , 4)
B	(2 , 3)	H	(9 , 4)
C	(2 , 4)	I	(9 , 3)
D	(5 , 4)	J	(13 , 3)
E	(5 , 6)	K	(11 , 1)
F	(7 , 6)	L	(2 , 1)
		M	(1 , 3)

AND HERE'S ANOTHER, IF YOU AREN'T ALREADY "DOG TIRED".

DOT'S OKAY!

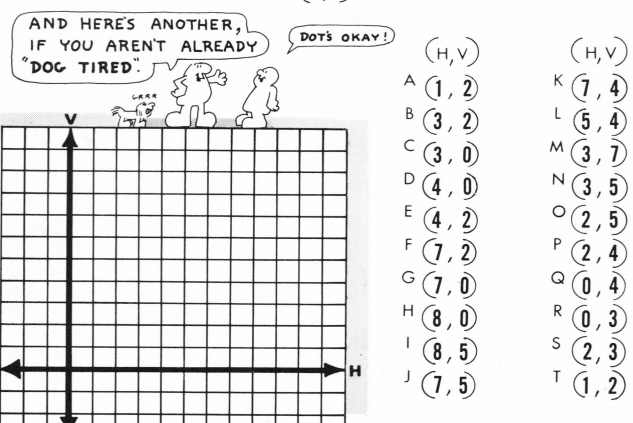

	(H , V)		(H , V)
A	(1 , 2)	K	(7 , 4)
B	(3 , 2)	L	(5 , 4)
C	(3 , 0)	M	(3 , 7)
D	(4 , 0)	N	(3 , 5)
E	(4 , 2)	O	(2 , 5)
F	(7 , 2)	P	(2 , 4)
G	(7 , 0)	Q	(0 , 4)
H	(8 , 0)	R	(0 , 3)
I	(8 , 5)	S	(2 , 3)
J	(7 , 5)	T	(1 , 2)

OK! SO THESE PICTURES AREN'T WORKS OF ART. WHY DON'T YOU DESIGN A PICTURE? WRITE DOWN THE ORDERED PAIRS AND EXCHANGE WITH A FRIEND.

EACH SMALL SQUARE IS ONE SQUARE UNIT.

FIND THE AREA OF EACH REGION.

BATTLESHIP

THE GAME OF **BATTLESHIP** IS A FUN GAME THAT PROVIDES LOTS OF PRACTICE IN PLOTTING COORDINATES.

ALL AHEAD FULL!

TWO PEOPLE PLAY THIS GAME. EACH PLAYER NEEDS A PIECE OF GRAPH PAPER WITH A HORIZONTAL AND VERTICAL AXIS DRAWN. PLAYERS AGREE ON HOW LARGE THEIR OCEAN (GRAPH PAPER) IS GOING TO BE.

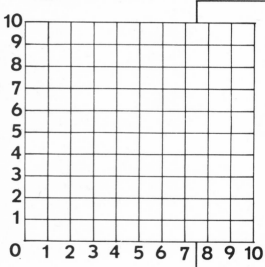

A 10X10 GRID IS A GOOD SIZE.

EACH PLAYER SECRETLY PLACES HIS FIVE SHIPS ON HIS SHEET OF PAPER.

SHIP SIZES ARE AS FOLLOWS:

		CIRCLES
BATTLESHIP:	5	○○○○○
CRUISER:	4	○○○○
DESTROYER:	3	○○○
SUBMARINE:	2	○○
TUG:	1	○

(CONTINUED)

BATTLESHIP

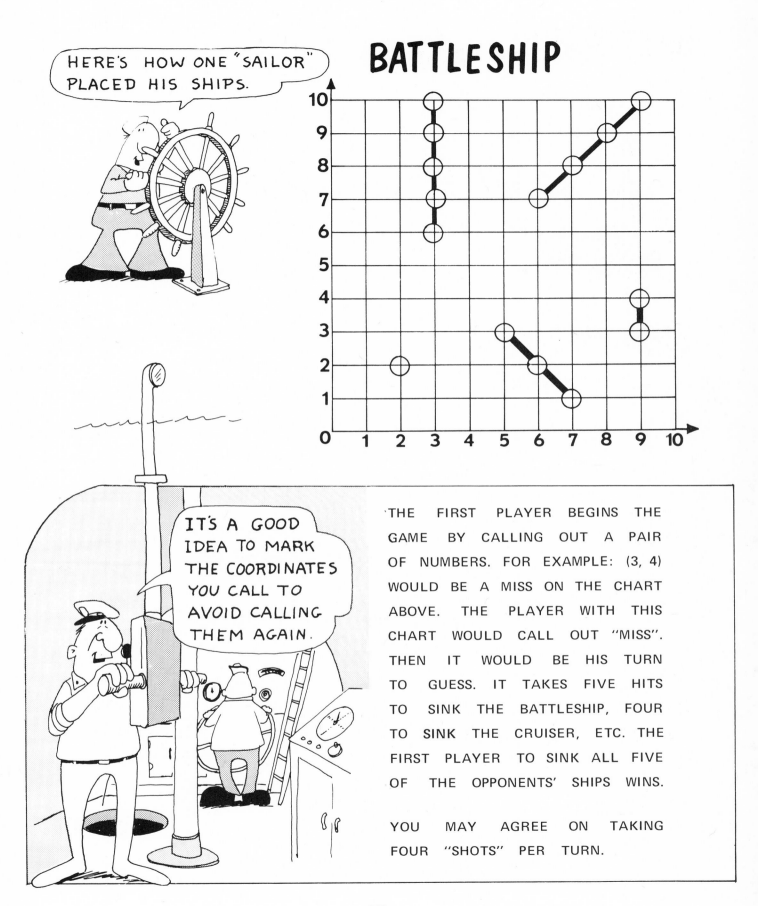

THE FIRST PLAYER BEGINS THE GAME BY CALLING OUT A PAIR OF NUMBERS. FOR EXAMPLE: (3, 4) WOULD BE A MISS ON THE CHART ABOVE. THE PLAYER WITH THIS CHART WOULD CALL OUT "MISS". THEN IT WOULD BE HIS TURN TO GUESS. IT TAKES FIVE HITS TO SINK THE BATTLESHIP, FOUR TO SINK THE CRUISER, ETC. THE FIRST PLAYER TO SINK ALL FIVE OF THE OPPONENTS' SHIPS WINS.

YOU MAY AGREE ON TAKING FOUR "SHOTS" PER TURN.

73

GUESSTIMATES

SEE HOW GOOD YOU ARE AT ESTIMATING THE MAP DISTANCES BELOW.

DANVILLE — 1 MI.
PECOS — 3 MI.
DALSEY — 15 MI.

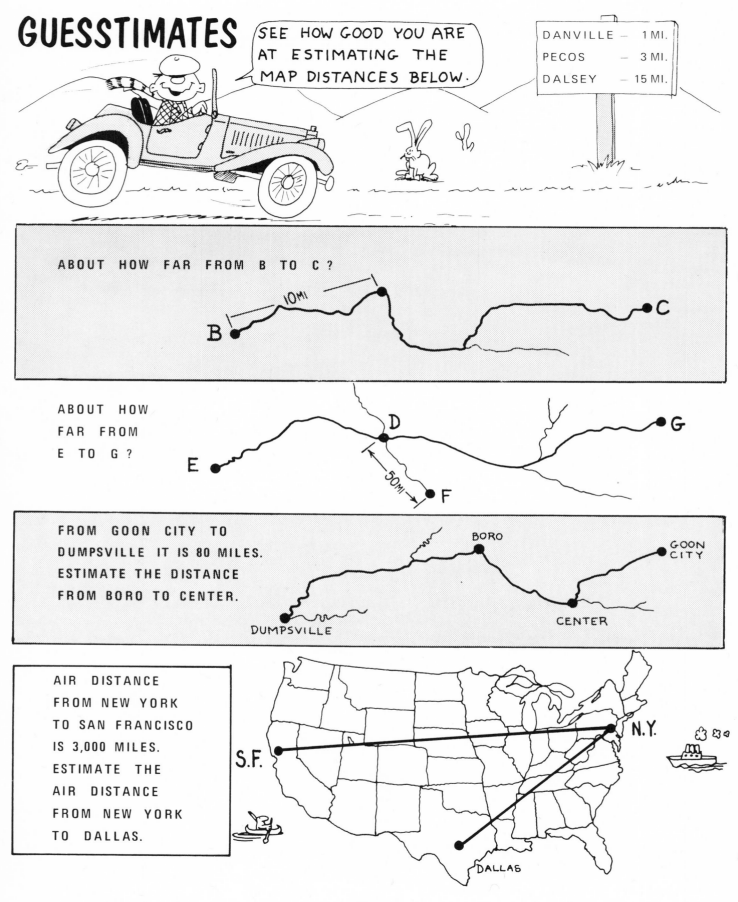

ABOUT HOW FAR FROM B TO C?

B — 10 MI — C

ABOUT HOW FAR FROM E TO G?

E — D — 50 MI — F — G

FROM GOON CITY TO DUMPSVILLE IT IS 80 MILES. ESTIMATE THE DISTANCE FROM BORO TO CENTER.

DUMPSVILLE — BORO — CENTER — GOON CITY

AIR DISTANCE FROM NEW YORK TO SAN FRANCISCO IS 3,000 MILES. ESTIMATE THE AIR DISTANCE FROM NEW YORK TO DALLAS.

S.F. — N.Y. — DALLAS

74

FIT THE

DISCS

ACROSS

AND

DOWN

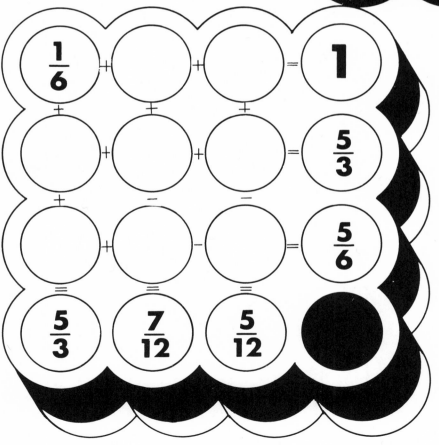

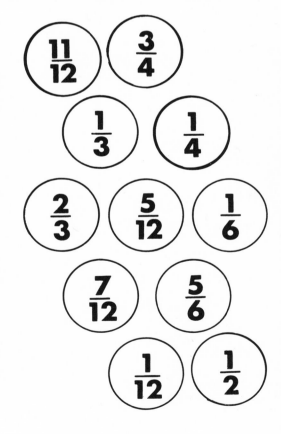

FRACTION TILES

SOME CAN BE DONE TWO WAYS.

USE TWO OF THESE TILES TO MAKE A TRUE SENTENCE.

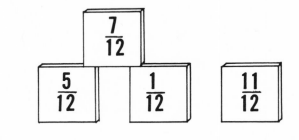

$\frac{7}{12}$ $\frac{5}{12}$ $\frac{1}{12}$ $\frac{11}{12}$

1) ☐ + ☐ = $1\frac{1}{3}$

2) ☐ − ☐ = $\frac{1}{2}$

3) ☐ + ☐ = $\frac{2}{3}$

4) ☐ + ☐ = 1

5) ☐ − ☐ = $\frac{1}{6}$

6) ☐ + ☐ = $\frac{1}{2}$

7) ☐ + ☐ = $1\frac{1}{2}$

8) ☐ − ☐ = $\frac{1}{3}$

HOW ABOUT USING ALL FOUR TILES?

9) ☐ + ☐ + ☐ + ☐ = ___

10) ☐ + ☐ − ☐ − ☐ = 0

76

HERE IS AN ANCIENT PUZZLE.

THERE THREE JUGS WHICH HOLD 8, 5, AND 3 LITRES. THE 8-LITRE JUG IS FULL AND THE OTHER TWO ARE EMPTY. HOW CAN YOU POUR FROM ONE JUG TO ANOTHER SO THAT THE WINE IS DIVIDED EVENLY IN TWO JUGS?

CAN YOU DO THIS IN NINE STEPS OR FEWER?

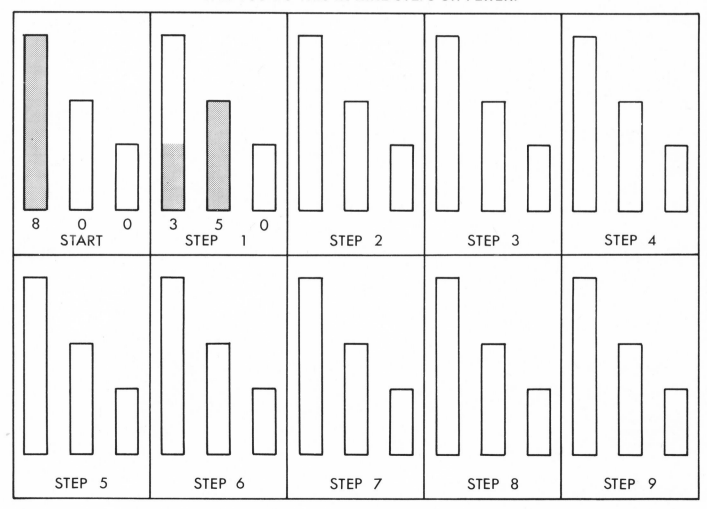

REMEMBERED BY THIS TRIANGLE:

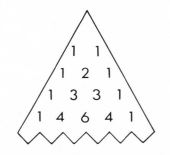

```
    1 1
   1 2 1
  1 3 3 1
 1 4 6 4 1
```

PROBABILITY CURVE

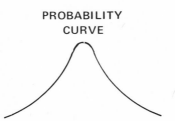

HE BECAME INTERESTED IN A <u>(1)</u> ROBLEM OF CHANCE WHILE ON A LONG JOURNEY. IT TOOK HIM TWO YEARS TO SOLVE THE PROBLEM. IT RESULTED IN THE DEVELOPMENT OF THE THEORY OF PROBABILITY.

AT THE <u>(2)</u> GE OF 12, HE DISCOVERED A GEOMETRY THEOREM OF HIS OWN.

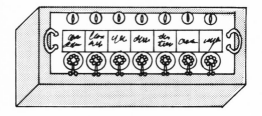

HE <u>(3)</u> TUDIED THE LAWS OF COMPRESSING AIR. HIS EXPERIMENTS LED TO THE DEVELOPMENT OF HYDRAULIC BRAKES.

HIS CONCISE ESSAY ON <u>(4)</u> ONICS, WRITTEN AT 16, CONTAINS CONTRIBUTIONS TO PROJECTIVE GEOMETRY.

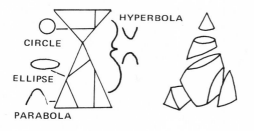

CIRCLE
ELLIPSE
PARABOLA
HYPERBOLA

AT 19, HE INVENTED AN <u>(5)</u> DDING MACHINE.

HIS LAW:

PRESSURE APPLIED TO ANY PART OF A CONFINED <u>(6)</u> IQUID IS TRANSMITTED UNCHANGED IN ALL DIRECTIONS.

1623 - 1662

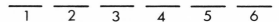

```
___ ___ ___ ___ ___ ___
 1   2   3   4   5   6
```

THIS ILLUSTRATION SHOWS HOW WE NUMBER THE ROWS IN

PASCAL'S TRIANGLE

$$1$$

ROW 1 $\longrightarrow$ 1 1

ROW 2 $\longrightarrow$ 1 ② 1

ROW 3 $\longrightarrow$ 1 ③ 3 1

ROW 4 $\longrightarrow$ 1 ④ 6 4 1

ROW 5 → 1 ⑤ __ __ __ __

FIND THE SUM OF EACH ROW IN PASCAL'S TRIANGLE AT THE RIGHT.

```
            1
         1     1        (1 + 1)           =  ____
       1    2    1      (1 + 2 + 1)       =  ____
     1    3    3    1   (1 + 3 + 3 + 1)   =  ____
   1    4    6    4    1                  =  ____
  1   5   10   10   5   1                 =  ____
 1   6   15   20   15   6   1             =  ____
1   7   21   35   35   21   7   1         =  ____
```

USING YOUR RESULTS ABOVE, FILL IN THESE BLANKS.

ROW	SUM		(EXPONENT FORM)
1	____	OR	2^1
2	____	OR	2^2
3	____	OR	2^3
4	____	OR	2^4
5	____	OR	____
6	____	OR	____
7	____	OR	____

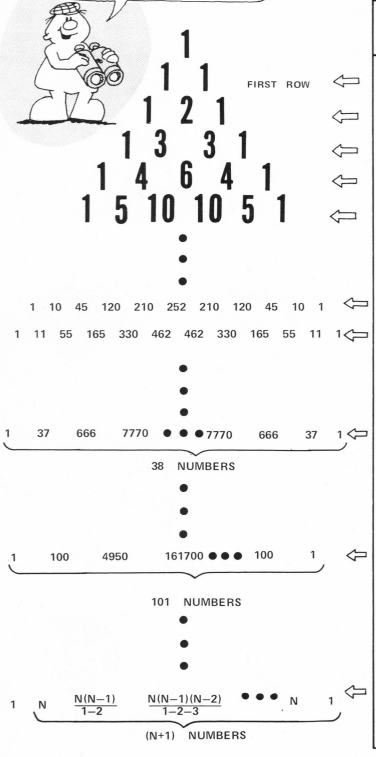

LOOK FOR PATTERNS TO COMPLETE THE TABLE BELOW:

FIRST ROW

38 NUMBERS

101 NUMBERS

(N+1) NUMBERS

ROW IN PASCAL'S TRIANGLE	SUM OF NUMBERS IN THAT ROW!
1	2^1
2	2^2
3	$2-$
4	$2-$
5	$2-$
•	•
10	$2-$
11	___
•	•
37	___
•	•
100	___
•	•
N	___

80

GOLDBACH'S CONJECTURE

IN 1742, THE GERMAN MATHEMATICIAN
C. GOLDBACH, MADE THE CONJECTURE
THAT EVERY EVEN NUMBER EXCEPT TWO
WAS THE SUM OF TWO PRIMES.

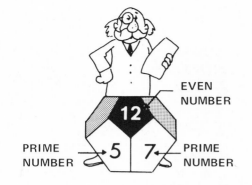

IN THE FIGURES BELOW, WRITE THE TWO
PRIMES THAT TOTAL THE EVEN NUMBER.

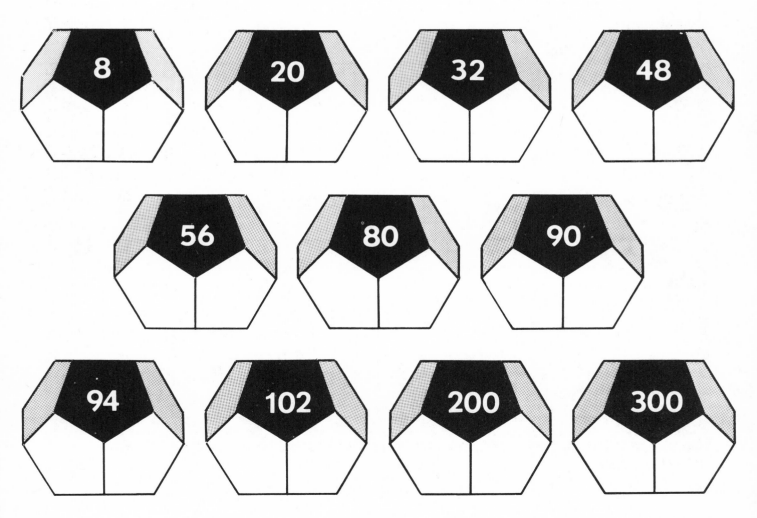

NAME GAME

CAN YOU FIND 25 DIFFERENT GEOMETRIC TERMS?

e	a	r	t	h	m	e	a	s	u	r	e
i	r	c	r	r	e	c	t	e	n	i	t
n	c	b	i	a	d	i	a	g	m	e	n
t	e	r	s	n	a	r	n	p	a	r	t
e	r	i	e	g	n	c	g	e	r	a	a
p	a	o	c	l	e	l	l	e	i	l	l
e	y	r	t	e	x	t	l	i	m	e	e
n	s	q	i	o	n	e	i	n	e	t	l
t	q	u	a	d	s	r	i	o	r	e	o
a	g	o	n	r	h	o	m	b	u	r	g
x	e	q	u	i	l	a	r	e	s	x	r
d	i	s	a	o	i	t	p	g	i	o	a
i	a	g	r	e	n	e	o	l	y	n	m
a	g	o	n	a	l	r	a	l	g	o	n

HORIZONTAL, VERTICAL, OR ZIG-ZAG

82

PLOTTING PICTURES

GRAPH THE FOLLOWING POINTS AND CONNECT EACH POINT
WITH THE NEXT POINT USING STRAIGHT LINE SEGMENTS.

CONNECT   (27 , 16) , (19 , 17) , (14 , 9) AND (19 , 2).

CONNECT   (14 , 9) , (5 , 11) , (3 , 6) , (2 , 13) , (3 , 22) , (5 , 20) AND (5 , 11).

CONNECT   (3 , 22) , (10 , 26) , (17 , 28) , (13 , 24) AND (5 , 20).

CONNECT   (17 , 28) , (25 , 23) , (27 , 16) , (27 , 7) , (19 , 2) , (12 , 1) AND (3 , 6).

FINALLY CONNECT   (13 , 24) AND (19 , 17).

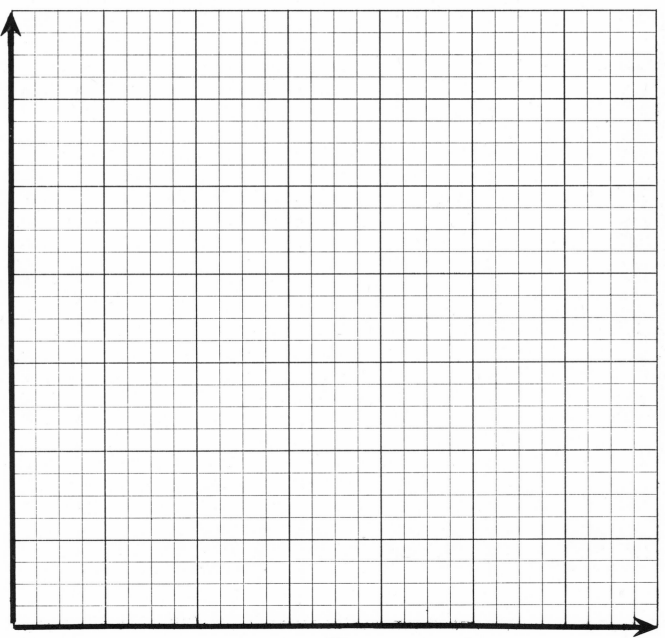

TILE TRIAL

USE ALL **FOUR** OF THESE TILES TO COMPLETE THE FOLLOWING SENTENCES.

EXAMPLE:

$$\triangle 5 \times \triangle 6 - \triangle 18 + \triangle 9 = 21$$

5

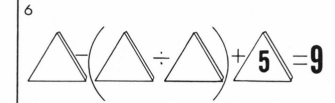
$$\triangle - \triangle + \triangle - \triangle 6 = 8$$

1

$$\triangle + (\triangle 18 \div \triangle) - \triangle = 1$$

6

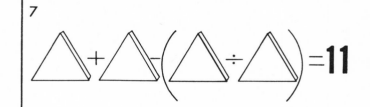
$$\triangle - (\triangle \div \triangle) + \triangle 5 = 9$$

2

$$\triangle + \triangle 5 + \triangle - \triangle = 2$$

7

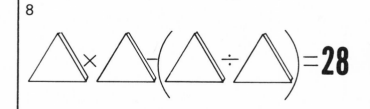
$$\triangle + \triangle - (\triangle \div \triangle) = 11$$

3

$$\triangle \div \triangle + \triangle - \triangle 5 = 3$$

8

$$\triangle \times \triangle - (\triangle \div \triangle) = 28$$

4

$$\triangle 18 \div \triangle + \triangle - \triangle = 7$$

DO OPERATIONS IN PARENTHESIS FIRST.... THEN PROCEED FROM LEFT TO RIGHT.

FIVE HATS

IN ANCIENT TIMES, FOUR MATHEMATICIANS DISCOVERED THIS GAME OF LOGIC. THE FOUR MEN WERE HERMOS, XENTOS, APPINO AND TENEDOS. HERMOS SEATED THE OTHER THREE MEN, ONE BEHIND THE OTHER, SO THAT XENTOS SAW APPINO AND TENEDOS, AND APPINO SAW ONLY TENEDOS. TENEDOS, WHO WAS IN FRONT, SAW NEITHER APPINO OR XENTOS.

HERMOS HAD FIVE HATS WHICH HE SHOWED TO THE THREE MEN. THREE OF THE HATS WERE GREY, AND TWO WERE WHITE. THEN HERMOS PUT A HAT ON EACH MAN AND TOSSED THE REMAINING TWO ASIDE.

"WHAT COLOR IS YOUR HAT XENTOS?" ASKED HERMOS. XENTOS DID NOT KNOW. APPINO DID NOT KNOW THE COLOR OF HIS HAT EITHER WHEN ASKED.

TENEDOS, WHO COULD NOT SEE ANY HATS AT ALL, GAVE THE RIGHT ANSWER WHEN HE WAS ASKED THE COLOR OF HIS HAT. WHAT WAS THE COLOR OF HIS HAT? HOW DID HE FIGURE IT OUT?

AVERAGES

AN AVERAGE IS THE SUM OF A SET OF NUMBERS DIVIDED BY THE NUMBER OF NUMBERS.

WHAT IS THE AVERAGE NOON TEMPERATURE IN SUN CITY?

MON	–	38°C
TUES	–	35°C
WED	–	40°C
THUR	–	28°C
SAT	–	33°C
SUN	–	36°C

WHAT IS THE AVERAGE NUMBER OF HEADS PER 100 TOSSES IN THESE THREE EXPERIMENTS?

EXPERIMENT 1
42 HEADS
58 TAILS

EXPERIMENT 2
46 HEADS
54 TAILS

EXPERIMENT 3
59 HEADS
41 TAILS

WHAT IS THE AVERAGE WEIGHT ON THE WRESTLING TEAM?

WRESTLING TEAM ROSTER

JONES	–	43 kg
GURST	–	47 kg
HOLMAN	–	51 kg
ERKS	–	56 kg
FLOOB	–	66 kg
MYER	–	73 kg
GRON	–	84 kg
B'AR	–	245 kg

ORDER SORTER

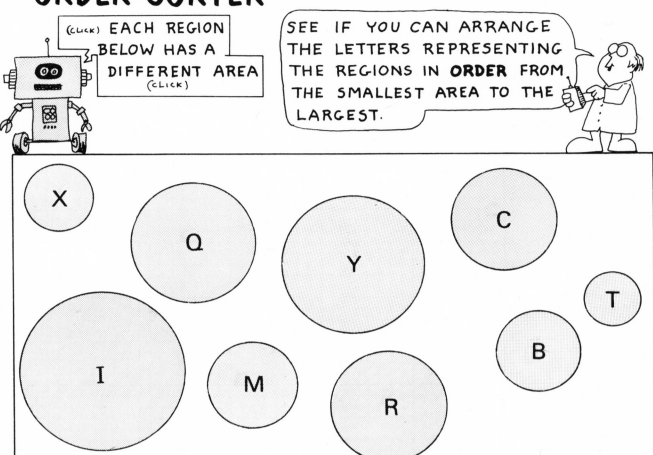

(CLICK) EACH REGION BELOW HAS A DIFFERENT AREA **(CLICK)**

SEE IF YOU CAN ARRANGE THE LETTERS REPRESENTING THE REGIONS IN **ORDER** FROM THE SMALLEST AREA TO THE LARGEST.

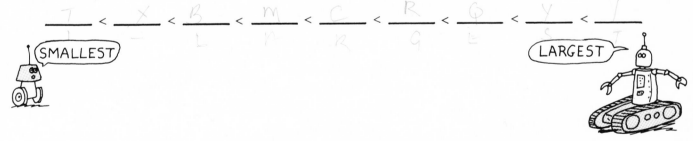

___ < ___ < ___ < ___ < ___ < ___ < ___ < ___ < ___

SMALLEST   LARGEST

USE THIS CHART TO DECODE THE LETTERS IN YOUR ANSWER ABOVE.

A	B	C	D	E	F	G	H	I	J	K	L	M	N	O	P	Q	R	S	T	U	V	W	X	Y	Z
D	L	R	B	U	J	N	Y	T	O	Q	H	A	V	M	W	E	G	P	I	X	C	K		S	F

_ _

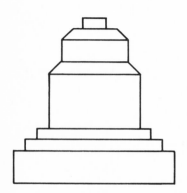

PROFILE PUZZLE

ONE OF THE SIXTEEN DRAWINGS BELOW IS THE CORRECT VIEW FROM THE TOP OF THE FIGURE AT THE LEFT.

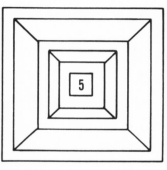 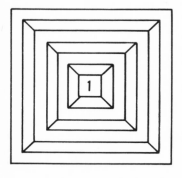 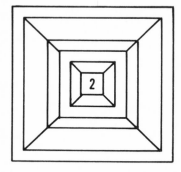 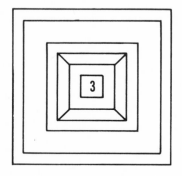 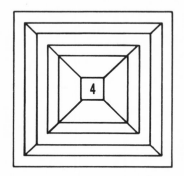 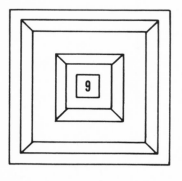 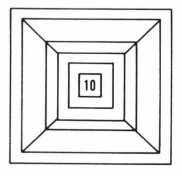 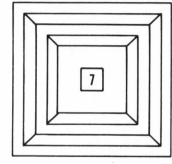 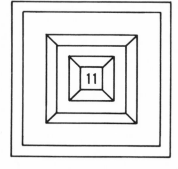 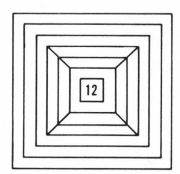 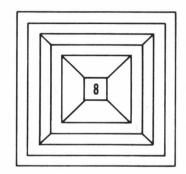  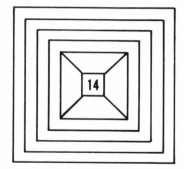 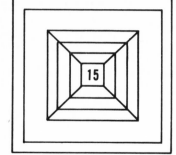 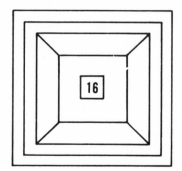

DESIGN VIA CODES

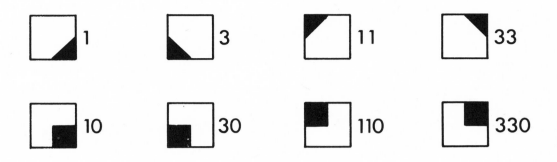

USE THE LEAST NUMBER OF SQUARES

1	40	40	4	40	40	4	40	40	3
340	0	0	0	0	0	0	0	0	140
340	0	120	0	34	14	0	360	0	140
34	0	0	120	33	11	360	0	0	14
340	0	4	3	120	330	1	4	0	140
340	0	44	11	30	120	33	44	0	140
34	0	0	360	1	3	120	0	0	14
340	0	360	0	34	14	0	120	0	140
340	0	0	0	0	0	0	0	0	140
33	440	440	44	440	440	44	440	440	11

COLORING POLYHEDRA

WOODLEY HAS JUST MADE A **DO—DECAHEDRON** MODEL. IT HAS 12 PENTAGONAL FACES. HE WANTS TO COLOR IT WITH FOUR COLORS.... RED, BLUE, GREEN AND YELLOW.

SHOWN BELOW ARE FLATTENED VIEWS OF THE 12 FACES. NO FACES WITH THE SAME COLOR SHOULD BE NEXT TO EACH OTHER. PART OF THE COLORING HAS BEEN DECIDED. CAN YOU COMPLETE IT?

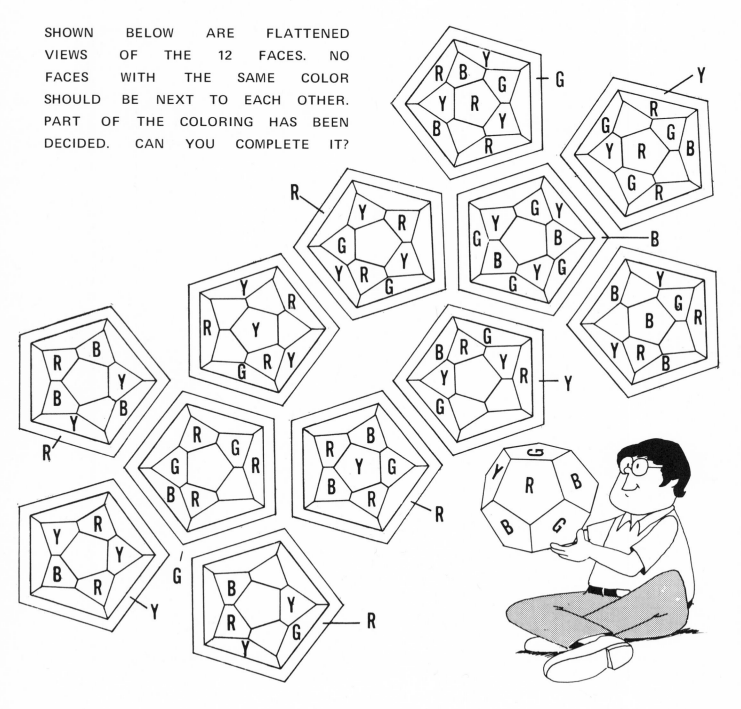

90

PEG PUZZLE PLANS

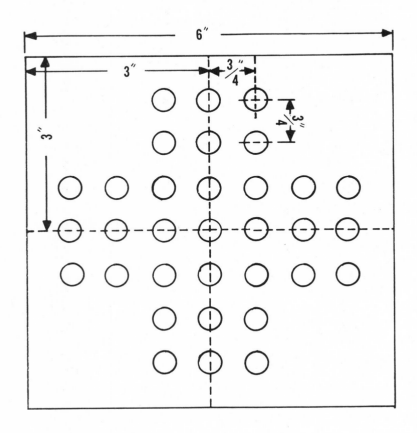

MATERIALS NEEDED:

ONE PIECE OF WOOD 6"X 6"X 1"
ONE DOWEL STICK (3/16" OR 1/4")
  36" LONG
QUARTER-INCH DRILL
HANDSAW AND SANDPAPER

CONSTRUCTION:

1) CUT BOARD IN A 6" SQUARE.
2) LAY OUT DESIGN AS SHOWN AT THE LEFT. MARK LOCATION ON HOLES ON THE BOARD.
3) DRILL HOLES A UNIFORM DEPTH. A 3/16" OR 1/4" DRILL BIT MAY BE BEST. DRILL SOME TEST HOLES IN A SCRAP BOARD TO SEE HOW THE DOWEL STICK FITS IN THE HOLE.
4) CUT 32 PEGS FROM YOUR DOWEL STICK THE DESIRED LENGTH.

RULES:

1) PLACE 32 PEGS ON THE BOARD, LEAVING THE CENTER HOLE OPEN.
2) EACH MOVE IS A JUMP IN A HORIZONTAL OR VERTICAL DIRECTION. EACH JUMPED PEG IS REMOVED FROM THE BOARD.
3) CONSECUTIVE JUMPS WITH ONE PEG ARE PERMITTED.
4) OBJECT IS TO REMOVE AS MANY PEGS FROM THE BOARD AS POSSIBLE.

PROPORTIONAL DRAWING

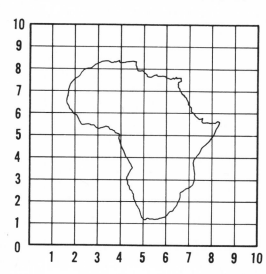

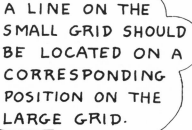

A LINE ON THE SMALL GRID SHOULD BE LOCATED ON A CORRESPONDING POSITION ON THE LARGE GRID.

MAKE AN ENLARGEMENT OF THE DRAWING AT THE LEFT ON THE GRID BELOW

THE AREA OF THE TWO DRAWINGS ARE IN THE RATIO OF 4 TO 1.

IF YOU DOUBLE THE DIMENSIONS YOU GET FOUR TIMES THE AREA.

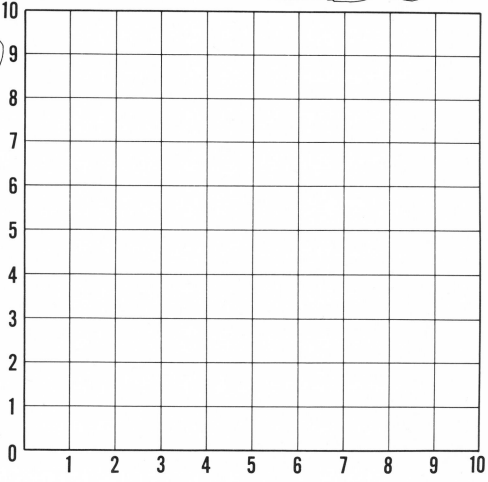

SOLID SHAPES

CUBE   DODECAHEDRON   PYRAMID   HEXAGONAL PRISM   CONE   RECTANGULAR PRISM   PARALLELEPIPED   TETRAHEDRON   SPHERE   CYLINDER   OCTAHEDRON   ICOSAHEDRON

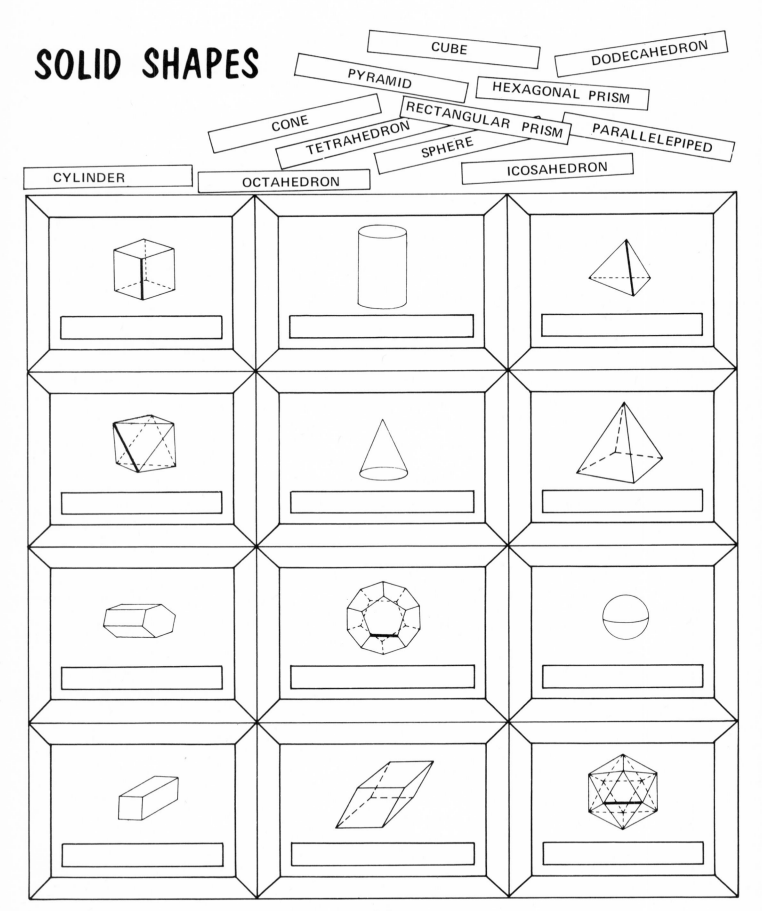

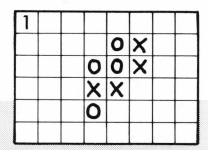

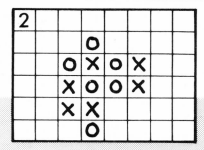

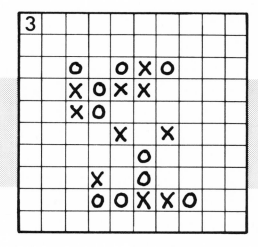

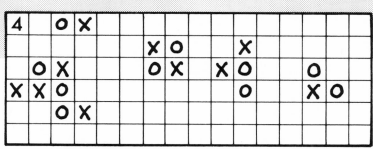

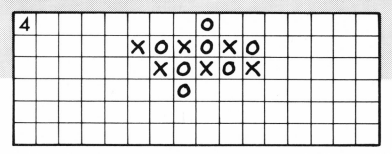

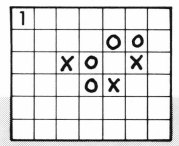

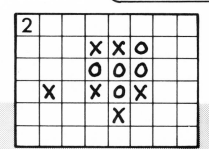

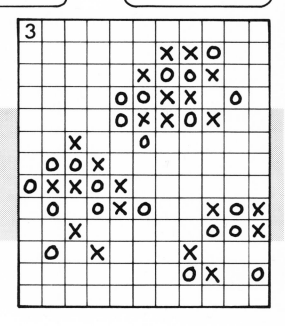

95

PATTERNS AND SEQUENCES

FIND THE PATTERN AND FILL IN THE MISSING NUMBERS.

1
9 — 18 — 27 — ◯ — ◯ — ◯ — ◯

2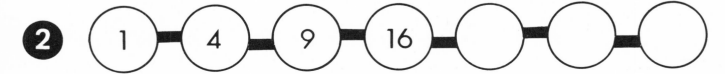
1 — 4 — 9 — 16 — ◯ — ◯ — ◯

3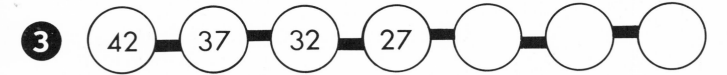
42 — 37 — 32 — 27 — ◯ — ◯ — ◯

4
1^0 — 1^1 — 1^2 — ◯ — ◯ — ◯ — ◯

5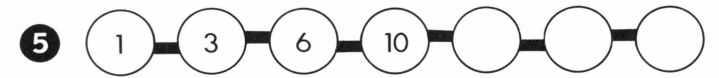
1 — 3 — 6 — 10 — ◯ — ◯ — ◯

6
10 — 5 — $2\frac{1}{2}$ — $1\frac{1}{4}$ — ◯ — ◯ — ◯

7
.03 — .06 — .09 — ◯ — ◯ — ◯ — ◯

8
1 — 1 — 2 — 3 — 5 — ◯ — ◯

9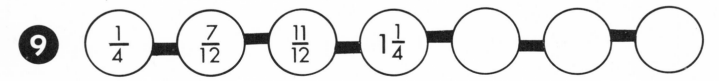
$\frac{1}{4}$ — $\frac{7}{12}$ — $\frac{11}{12}$ — $1\frac{1}{4}$ — ◯ — ◯ — ◯

ACCURACY

IN ORDER TO GET THE CORRECT ANSWER TO THE DIVISION PROBLEM BELOW, YOU MUST DO MANY CALCULATIONS. ONE MISTAKE WILL RESULT IN A WRONG ANSWER. HOW IS YOUR ACCURACY? CAN YOU FIND THE CORRECT QUOTIENT THE FIRST TIME?

CHECK POINTS:
There is no remainder.
The third difference is 68448.
Every digit except 4 appears exactly once in the quotient.

$$8459 \overline{)3069002811325}$$

SOMETIMES ACCURACY IS BETTER THAN SPEED!

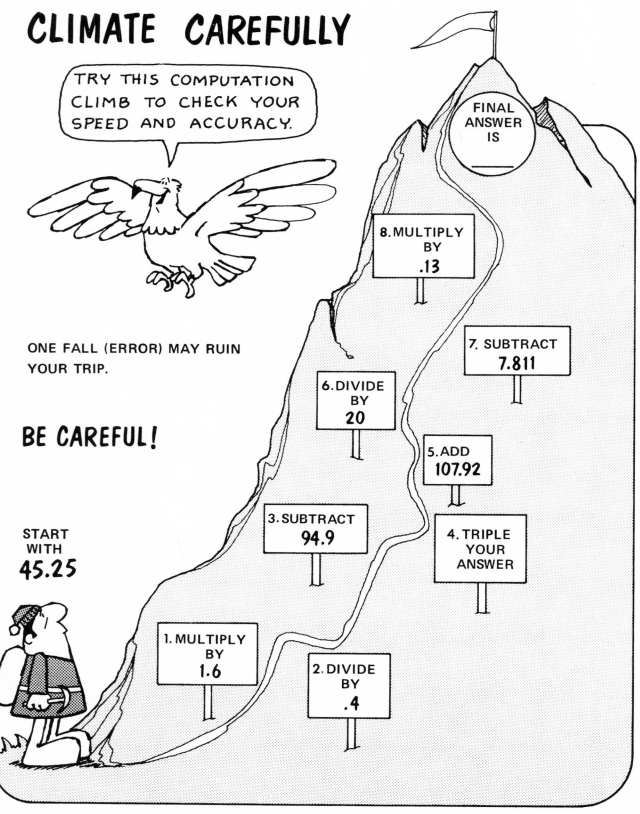

CLIMATE CAREFULLY

TRY THIS COMPUTATION CLIMB TO CHECK YOUR SPEED AND ACCURACY.

FINAL ANSWER IS
_____

8. MULTIPLY BY .13

7. SUBTRACT 7.811

ONE FALL (ERROR) MAY RUIN YOUR TRIP.

6. DIVIDE BY 20

5. ADD 107.92

BE CAREFUL!

3. SUBTRACT 94.9

4. TRIPLE YOUR ANSWER

START WITH 45.25

1. MULTIPLY BY 1.6

2. DIVIDE BY .4

99

DRIBBLE DERBY

THE FIVE STARTING PLAYERS ON THE CENTRAL BASKET-BALL TEAM ARE: "DUNKIN" DAN, "PIVOTING" PETE, "EL-BOWING" ED, "JUMPIN" JOE, AND "SMOOTH" SAM.

1. TWO OF THESE PLAYERS WEAR WHITE SHOES AND THREE WEAR BLACK SHOES.
2. THREE ARE FORWARDS AND TWO ARE GUARDS. (YOU'RE RIGHT — NO CENTER!)
3. "DUNKIN" DAN AND "JUMPIN" JOE WEAR THE SAME COLOR SHOES.
4. "SMOOTH" SAM AND "ELBOWING" ED WEAR DIFFER-ENT COLORED SHOES.
5. PETE AND ED PLAY THE SAME POSITION.
6. JOE AND SAM PLAY DIFFERENT POSITIONS.
7. THE GUARD WHO WEARS WHITE SHOES IS THE LEADING SCORER ON THE TEAM.

WHAT IS HIS NAME?

DIGIT DISCOVERY

PHOTO ALBUM PAGES

CAN YOU PLACE THESE SNAPSHOTS ON THE PHOTO ALBUM PAGES?

1

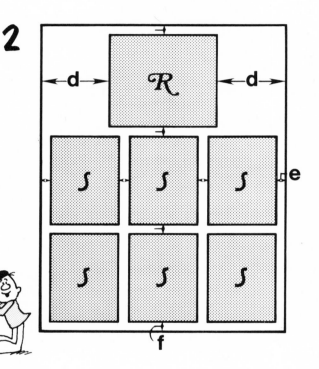

1. Album page: 12″ x 18″

   Q: 3″ x 4″

   Find: a = _____″, b = _____″,

   c = _____″.

2

IT MAY BE HELPFUL TO MAKE A MODEL OF THESE ALBUM PAGES.

3

2. Album page: 27 cm x 35 cm

   R: 12 cm wide x 10.6 cm high

   S: 7.8 cm x 10.2 cm

   Find: d = _____ cm, e = _____ cm,

   f = _____ cm

3. Album page: $11\frac{1}{4}$″ x 17″

   T: $2\frac{3}{4}$″ x $3\frac{1}{2}$″

   Find: g = _____″, h = _____″,

   i = _____″.

PHOTO ALBUM PAGES

1. Album page: 20 cm x 30 cm

   U: 14 cm x 9 cm

   V: 6.4 cm x 8 cm

   Find: j = _____ cm, k = _____ cm,

   $\quad\quad$ l = _____ cm

2. Album page: 15″ x 22″

   W: $2\frac{1}{2}$″ high x 3″ wide

   X: 5″ x 7″

   Find: m = _____″, n = _____″,

   $\quad\quad$ p = _____″, q = _____″

3. Album page: 36 cm x 56 cm

   Y: 14 cm x 10 cm $\quad\quad$ A: 25 cm x 19 cm

   Z: 19 cm x 13 cm

   Find: r = _____ cm, s = _____ cm,

   $\quad\quad$ t = _____ cm, u = _____ cm

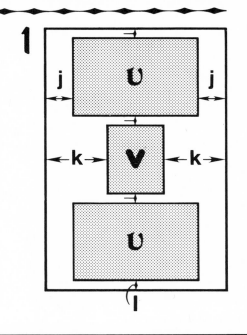

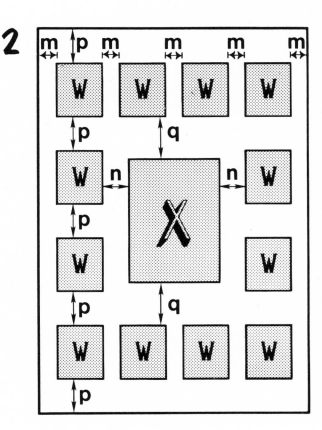

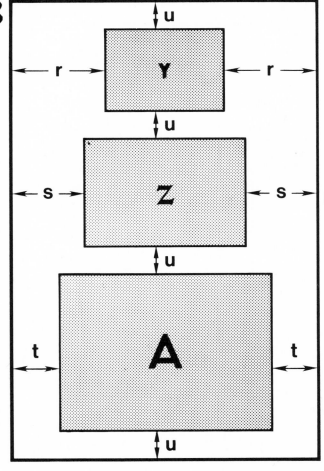

RANDOM DIGIT ACTIVITIES

I. FACTOR BINGO I

Draw a border around a square of 25 digits to use as a Bingo card. The teacher or a student rolls two dice and calls out the sum of the faces. Write the sum over one of its multiples. A factor can only be written over one number in a turn. The first player to write over five numbers in a column *and* a row wins.

VARIATIONS: a) Play black out, requiring that all 25 numbers must be written over to win the game.

b) Draw a border around a single row or column to use as a Bingo card.

c) Black out two numbers at a time if they are adjacent and have common multiples. For example, **35 7 28**

II. FACTOR CHAIN PUZZLES

Make a common factor chain across the page from one corner to another. Do not connect numbers in a diagonal chain.

VARIATIONS: a) Make a chain across the page in the middle.

b) Make a chain from the top of the page to the bottom.

c) Make the longest vertical chain of common factors that you can. Is it as long as the longest horizontal chain that you can make?

III. FACTOR BINGO II

Draw a border around a row on the random digit page to use as a Bingo card. The teacher or a student rolls a die (or spins a spinner) and calls out the number. Write this number between two adjacent numbers of which it is a factor. The first player to connect a complete row wins. Remember, one is a factor of every number.

Examples,

$24\ ^3 15$ OK $24\ ^6 12$ OK

$24\ ^1 15$ OK $49\ ^1 36$ OK

If you liked these activities you may wish to try the random digit activities in *Aftermath I* and *II* or the Hidden Products activity in *Aftermath IV*. Make up some games of your own.

RANDOM DIGIT PAGE

	1	2	3	4	5	6	7	8	9	10	11	12	13	14	15	16	17	18
25	12	42	36	24	60	5	36	54	16	50	33	27	48	32	7	66	40	56
24	40	3	48	84	12	35	20	30	24	4	88	8	40	21	16	49	18	2
23	24	32	10	18	60	28	6	44	10	60	18	36	12	63	30	9	81	15
22	6	77	25	49	14	81	48	27	96	25	40	9	88	3	64	24	30	12
21	96	36	70	4	72	22	56	8	32	16	55	11	54	24	10	6	45	66
20	45	8	15	55	9	18	7	21	72	2	20	81	12	90	36	14	20	33
19	20	88	27	24	50	12	77	36	24	10	48	30	4	42	9	48	80	22
18	56	49	11	54	5	84	35	4	20	96	36	24	48	30	50	16	4	72
17	30	4	80	20	64	10	44	80	14	8	63	5	88	36	25	99	18	40
16	48	50	6	22	40	33	60	12	77	30	40	33	6	40	2	36	72	24
15	36	12	21	66	2	25	16	9	44	33	10	55	24	54	7	16	12	90
14	64	30	7	16	48	24	42	20	3	72	36	12	33	11	45	20	56	15
13	9	55	18	81	36	6	49	30	66	15	49	4	30	96	10	60	6	36
12	35	24	60	8	28	48	10	24	5	64	22	81	21	8	66	14	72	12
11	60	3	20	48	14	36	30	8	56	40	9	16	63	27	32	9	35	3
10	18	99	36	4	90	9	45	35	11	24	80	4	36	12	72	36	24	99
9	63	16	10	63	21	70	12	2	60	28	20	60	18	54	6	80	11	64
8	50	9	40	25	6	24	32	18	12	6	50	8	66	16	4	22	55	5
7	15	88	5	22	42	12	96	7	70	27	36	10	42	14	77	30	20	90
6	36	24	72	11	28	70	20	49	12	44	3	32	88	9	36	2	40	9
5	99	7	27	96	18	8	54	16	48	18	90	24	6	72	15	45	10	72
4	44	12	14	2	30	90	15	84	4	63	10	20	56	12	55	18	42	8
3	25	84	24	81	9	6	77	11	40	22	12	77	28	60	7	70	16	5
2	66	4	45	16	64	10	24	72	3	32	72	8	21	4	44	6	24	88
1	24	80	12	54	36	20	12	8	60	42	24	40	12	49	27	56	72	48

SOLUTIONS

BOOK THREE

CELEBRATION, Pages 1–2

Numbers honored are one and zero.

STAR SEARCH, Page 3

1)	5	6)	3
2)	19	7)	0
3)	1	8)	1
4)	5	9)	1
5)	2	10)	3

MULTIBASE CHART, Page 5

2	6	3
7	10	8

DESIGN MATRIX PUZZLE, Page 6

MATH PUN FUN, Page 7

AREA	VOLUME	LENGTH
METER	INCHES	MEASURE

<u>R U L E R S</u>

ADD–SUB SLIDE RULE, Page 9–10

1) 5_7	5) 15_7	9) 3_7	13) 6_7
2) 10_7	6) 15_7	10) 1_7	14) 10_7
3) 11_7	7) 15_7	11) 3_7	
4) 5_7	8) 20_7	12) 6_7	

MOVING MATCHES, Page 11

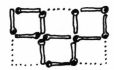

DIVISIBILITY, Page 12

a) 8, 10, 12   e) 9, 10, 12
b) 8, 10   f) 10, 12
c) 8, 12   g) 9, 10
d) 12   h) 9

ARROWMATH, Pages 14—15

1) Yes
2) No
3) Addition
4) Multiplication

① **6 →** = __7__   ⑤ **16 ⫽⫽** = __4__

② **8 ↓→** = __14__   ⑥ **7 →←** = __7__

③ **9 ↗↓** = __10__   ⑦ **12 ⫽⫽** = __12__

④ **13 ↘↑** = __2__   ⑧ **18 ↑↓** = __18__

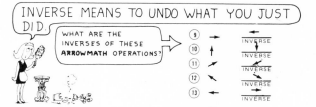

INVERSE MEANS TO UNDO WHAT YOU JUST DID.

WHAT ARE THE INVERSES OF THESE **ARROWMATH** OPERATIONS?

⑨ → — INVERSE ←
⑩ ↑ — INVERSE ↓
⑪ ↗ — INVERSE ↙
⑫ ↘ — INVERSE ↗
⑬ ← — INVERSE →

HOW MANY ?, Page 16

Pentagons: 18
Squares: 31
Composites: 13
License Plates 3^3 or 27

MONEY MATCHING, Page 17

$ 1   Washington
$ 2   Jefferson
$ 5   Lincoln
$ 10   Hamilton
$ 20   Jackson
$ 50   Grant
$ 100   Franklin

MULTIPLE MAGIC, Page 18—19

B) 9 or 1   C) 4 or 6   D) 5
E) 2 or 8   F) 4 or 6

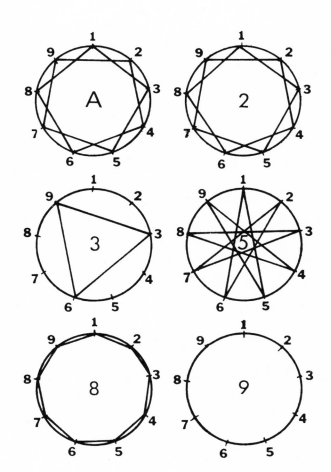

COIN CAPERS, Page 21

A) Hold the nickel and either force the penny between the nickel and the dime or hit the nickel with the penny causing the dime to move away from the nickel.

B) 12 pennies.

C) Always fill the vertex that you have just moved from so that you don't fill two vertices from the same point.

A WHOLE THING, Page 23

1	2
a) 1/4	a) 1/2
b) 2 1/2	b) 5
c) 1 1/2	c) 3
d) 2 3/4	

WHICH ONE DIFFERS?, Page 24

1) E   2) B   3) E   4) C   5) B

EQUATION PUZZLE, Page 26

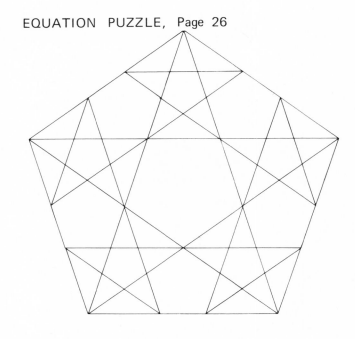

HOW BIG IS TEN MILLION?, Page 27

Miami to Washington

POLYHEDRA PUZZLE, Page 28

SPAGHETTI MAZE, Page 32

1 — 6, 2 — 4, 3 — 5

I AM A NUMBER GAME, Page 33

Top: 180
Bottom: 1537

LINE DESIGN, Page 34

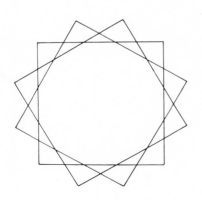

LINE DESIGN, Page 34 (cont.)

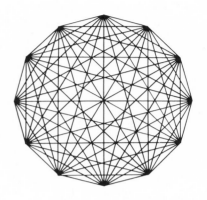

PRIME FACTOR TENTS, Page 35

NUMBER PATTERNS, Page 36

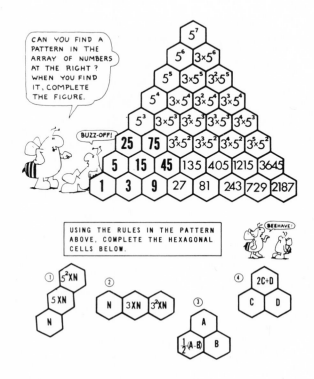

HOW MANY ?, Page 37

Triangles:	47
Prime Numbers:	9
Segments:	10
Angles:	10

TILE TRIAL, Page 38

Answers not unique

1) $5 \times 8 - 40 = 0$
2) $5 - 40 \div 10 = 1$
3) $5 + 8 - 10 = 3$
4) $8 \div (10 \div 5) = 4$
5) $10 - 8 + 5 = 7$
6) $40 \div 10 + 5 = 9$
7) $10 \div 5 + 8 = 10$
8) $10 \div 5 \times 8 = 16$

AREA AND PERIMETER, Page 39

Areas may range from 128 for 4 × 32 rectangle to 324 for 18 × 18. Shape for maximum area is a square.

GIVING DIRECTIONS, Page 40

This is intended to be a class discussion exercise.

TINKERTOTALS, Page 46

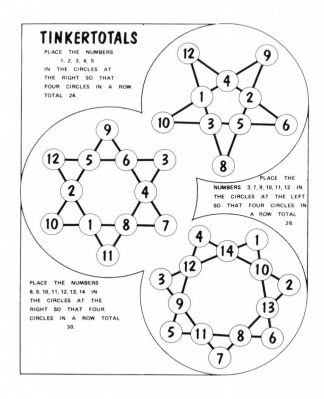

SOLUTIONS

FIND MY PATTERN, Page 47

0	7	2
8	3	4
9	5	1

TRELLIS TWISTER, Page 48

Number 6.

CONSTELLATION AREAS, Page 50

1) 2	9) 3 1/2
2) 2	10) 3
3) 3	11) 1 1/2
4) 3	12) 1 1/2
5) 2 1/2	13) 3
6) 2	14) 3
7) 4	15) 8
8) 3 1/2	16) 7 1/2

LOGIC LURE, Page 51

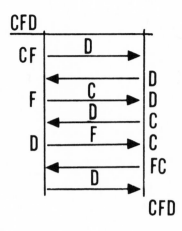

I AM A NUMBER GAME, Page 52

Top: 90
Bottom: 70

PENTAGONAL ARITHMETIC, Page 53

"+"	△	Z	⊖	#	□
△	△	Z	⊖	#	□
Z	Z	⊖	#	□	△
⊖	⊖	#	□	△	Z
#	#	□	△	Z	⊖
□	□	△	Z	⊖	#

PENTAGONAL ARITHMETIC, Page 53 (cont.)

"×"	△	Z	⊖	#	□
△	△	△	△	△	△
Z	△	Z	⊖	#	□
⊖	△	⊖	□	Z	#
#	△	#	Z	□	⊖
□	△	□	#	⊖	Z

Z　acts like one.

△　acts like zero.

NILE TILE, Page 54

These answers may not be unique.

1. $\frac{5}{6}$ = ⌓ + ⬯

2. $\frac{1}{2}$ = ⌓ − ⬯

3. $\frac{2}{3}$ = ⬯ + ⬯

4. $\frac{7}{12}$ = ⬯ + ⬯

5. $\frac{3}{4}$ = ⊏ + ⬯

6. $\frac{5}{12}$ = ⌓ − ⬯

7. $\frac{3}{4}$ = ⬯ + ⬯ + ⬯

8. $\frac{7}{12}$ = ⊏ + ⬯ − ⬯

FIBONACCI SEQUENCE MAZE, Page 55

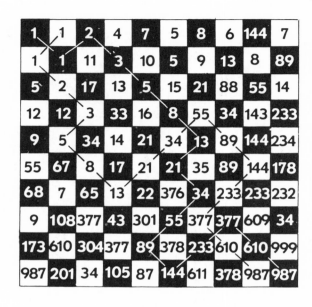

1	1	2	4	7	5	8	6	144	7
1	1	11	3	10	5	9	13	8	89
5	2	17	13	5	15	21	88	55	14
12	12	3	33	16	8	55	34	143	233
9	5	34	14	21	34	13	89	144	234
55	67	8	17	21	21	35	89	144	178
68	7	65	13	22	376	34	233	233	232
9	108	377	43	301	55	377	377	609	34
173	610	304	377	89	378	233	610	610	999
987	201	34	105	87	144	611	378	987	987

PUZZLERS, Page 58

Top:　Cut each link of one chain and use them to connect the remaining 5 chains.

Middle:

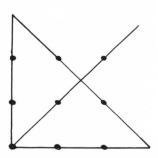

Bottom:

	100	164
	125	125
	225 or 15^2	289 or 17^2

TRANSYLVANIA TRANSITIVITY, Page 59

From left to right:
Ted, Red, Al, Ned, Sal, Ike, Todd, Ian, Van, and Ed.   Initials spell
<u>T R A N S I T I V E</u>.

LOGIC, Page 60

1) 5   3) 4   5) 1   7) 1
2) 2   4) 4   6) 5

WHICH ONE DIFFERS?, Page 61

A) 4   B) 3   C) 3   D) 2   E) 1

WHAT'S MY WORD?, Page 64

C O R N F L A K E S

PENTOMINO PUZZLE, Page 65

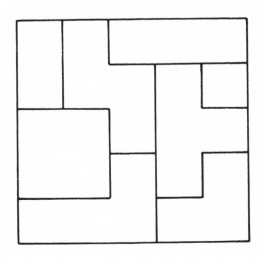

PENTOMINO PUZZLE, Page 65 (cont.)

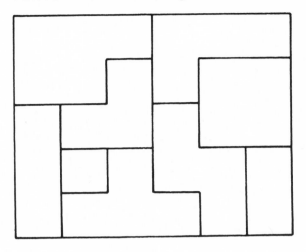

PRIME MAZE, Page 66

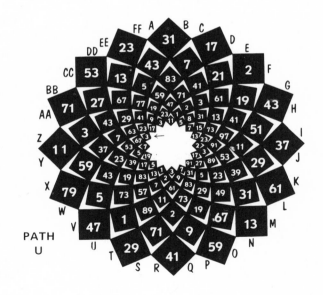

CODE MODE, Page 67

Message: One small step for a man,
one giant leap for mankind.

PLOTTING POINTS, Page 70

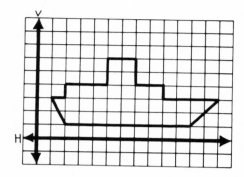

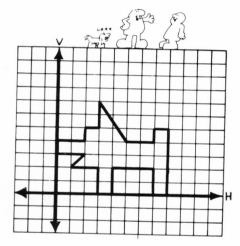

NUMERAL AREA, Page 71

1) 24 1/2   6) 66
2) 49 1/2   7) 13
3) 50   8) 71
4) 40 1/2   9) 121
5) 54 1/2

GUESSTIMATES, Page 74

B to C: about 30 miles
E to G: about 300 miles
Boro to Center: about 20 miles
New York to Dallas: about 1700 miles

FIT THE DISCS, Page 75

$$1 + \frac{5}{6} + \frac{3}{4} = \frac{31}{12}$$
$$+ \qquad + \qquad +$$
$$\frac{1}{12} + \frac{1}{4} + \frac{7}{12} = \frac{11}{12}$$
$$+ \qquad + \qquad +$$
$$\frac{5}{12} + \frac{1}{3} + \frac{1}{2} = \frac{5}{4}$$
$$= \qquad = \qquad =$$
$$\frac{3}{2} \qquad \frac{17}{12} \qquad \frac{11}{6} \qquad \blacksquare$$

$$\frac{1}{6} + \frac{3}{4} + \frac{1}{12} = 1$$
$$+ \qquad + \qquad +$$
$$\frac{7}{12} + \frac{1}{4} + \frac{5}{6} = \frac{5}{3}$$
$$+ \qquad - \qquad -$$
$$\frac{11}{12} + \frac{5}{12} - \frac{1}{2} = \frac{5}{6}$$
$$= \qquad = \qquad =$$
$$\frac{5}{3} \qquad \frac{7}{12} \qquad \frac{5}{12} \qquad \blacksquare$$

Answers not unique.

FRACTION TILES, Page 76

1) 11/12 + 5/12 = 1 1/3
2) 11/12 − 5/12 = 1/2
3) 7/12 + 1/12 = 2/3
4) 7/12 + 5/12 = 1
5) 7/12 − 5/12 = 1/6
6) 5/12 + 1/12 = 1/2
7) 7/12 + 11/12 = 1 1/2
8) 5/12 − 1/12 = 1/3
9) 7/12 + 11/12 + 5/12 + 1/12 = 2
10) 7/12 + 5/12 − 1/12 − 11/12 = 0

ANCIENT PUZZLE, Page 77

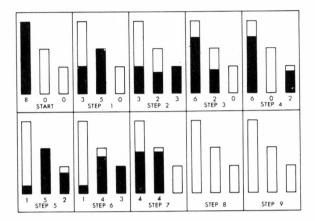

8 0 0	3 5 0	3 2 3	6 2 0	6 0 2
START	STEP 1	STEP 2	STEP 3	STEP 4

1 5 2	1 4 3	4 4		
STEP 5	STEP 6	STEP 7	STEP 8	STEP 9

FAMOUS MATHEMATICIAN, Page 78

P A S C A L

PASCAL'S TRIANGLE, Page 79

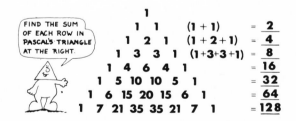

FIND THE SUM OF EACH ROW IN PASCAL'S TRIANGLE AT THE RIGHT.

```
            1
          1   1      (1 + 1)      =   2
        1   2   1    (1 + 2 + 1)  =   4
      1   3   3   1  (1+3+3+1)    =   8
    1   4   6   4   1             =  16
  1   5  10  10   5   1           =  32
1   6  15  20  15   6   1         =  64
1  7  21  35  35  21   7   1      = 128
```

USING YOUR RESULTS ABOVE, FILL IN THESE BLANKS.

ROW	SUM		(EXPONENT FORM)
1	2	OR	2^1
2	4	OR	2^2
3	8	OR	2^3
4	16	OR	2^4
5	32	OR	2^5
6	64	OR	2^6
7	128	OR	2^7

PASCAL'S TRIANGLE, Page 80

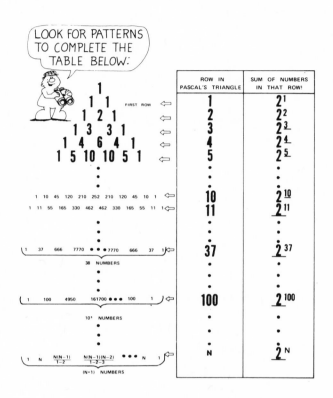

LOOK FOR PATTERNS TO COMPLETE THE TABLE BELOW:

ROW IN PASCAL'S TRIANGLE	SUM OF NUMBERS IN THAT ROW!
1	2^1
2	2^2
3	2^3
4	2^4
5	2^5
·	·
10	2^{10}
11	2^{11}
·	·
37	2^{37}
·	·
100	2^{100}
·	·
N	2^N

GOLDBACH'S CONJECTURE, Page 81

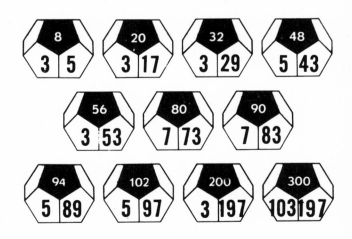

8	20	32	48
3 5	3 17	3 29	5 43

56	80	90
3 53	7 73	7 83

94	102	200	300
5 89	5 97	3 197	103 197

115

NAME GAME, Page 82

CAN YOU FIND 25 DIFFERENT GEOMETRIC TERMS?

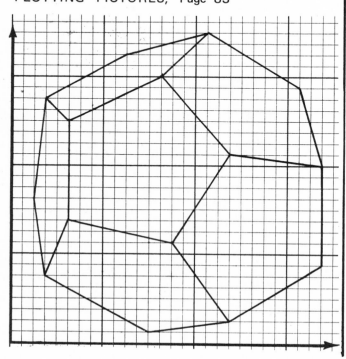

PLOTTING PICTURES, Page 83

TILE TRIAL, Page 84

1) $5 + (18 \div 9) - 6 = 1$
2) $9 + 5 + 6 - 18 = 2$
3) $18 \div 9 + 6 - 5 = 3$
4) $18 \div 6 + 9 - 5 = 7$
5) $18 - 9 + 5 - 6 = 8$
6) $6 - (18 \div 9) + 5 = 9$
7) $9 + 5 - (18 \div 6) = 11$
8) $6 \times 5 - (18 \div 9) = 28$

FIVE HATS, Page 85

Since Xentos answered no, both hats in front could not have been white. Hence either G, G; W, G; or G, W. If the hats were W, G then Appino would have known the color of his hat. Hence, Tenedos' hat must have been grey.

AVERAGES, Page 86

Average temperature:	35°C
Average number of heads:	49
Average weight:	83.125 kg

ORDER SORTER, Page 87

$T < X < B < M < C < R < Q < Y < I$

I   L A R G E S T

PROFILE PUZZLE, Page 88

  Number 12.

DESIGN VIA CODES, Page 89

COLORING POLYHEDRA, Page 90

SOLID SHAPES, Page 94

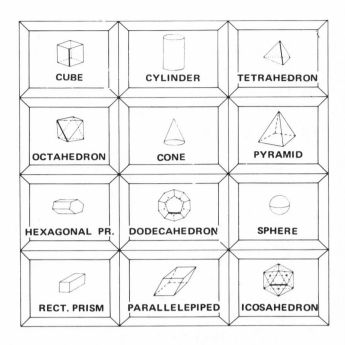

FIVE—IN—A—ROW, Page 95

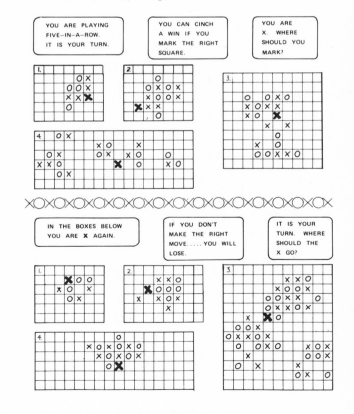

PATTERNS AND SEQUENCES, Page 96

1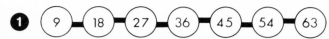
9 — 18 — 27 — 36 — 45 — 54 — 63

2
1 — 4 — 9 — 16 — 25 — 36 — 49

3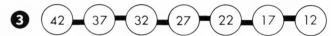
42 — 37 — 32 — 27 — 22 — 17 — 12

4
1^0 — 1^1 — 1^2 — 1 — 1 — 1 — 1

5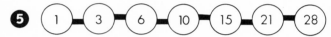
1 — 3 — 6 — 10 — 15 — 21 — 28

6
10 — 5 — $2\frac{1}{2}$ — $1\frac{1}{4}$ — $\frac{5}{8}$ — $\frac{5}{16}$ — $\frac{5}{32}$

7
.03 — .06 — .09 — .12 — .15 — .18 — .21

8
1 — 1 — 2 — 3 — 5 — 8 — 13

9
$\frac{1}{4}$ — $\frac{7}{12}$ — $\frac{11}{12}$ — $1\frac{1}{4}$ — $1\frac{7}{12}$ — $1\frac{11}{12}$ — $2\frac{1}{4}$

ACCURACY, Page 97

362, 809, 175

CLIMATE CAREFULLY, Page 98

1.365

WHAT'S MY NAME?, Page 99

A. $\frac{1}{8}$ B. $\frac{3}{5}$ C. $\frac{2}{7}$

DRIBBLE DERBY, Page 100

Sam

DIGIT DISCOVERY, Page 101

4	7	2
0	6	8
9	1	5

PHOTO ALBUM PAGES, Page 102

1. a = 2″, b = $4\frac{1}{2}$″, c = $1\frac{1}{2}$″
2. d = 7.5 cm, e = 0.9 cm, f = 1.0 cm
3. g = $\frac{3}{4}$″, h = $4\frac{1}{4}$″, i = $1\frac{5}{8}$″

PHOTO ALBUM PAGES, Page 103

1. j = 3 cm, k = 6.8 cm, l = 1.0 cm
2. m = 1″, n = $1\frac{1}{2}$″, p = 2″, q = $2\frac{1}{2}$″
3. r = 11 cm, s = 8.5 cm, t = 5.5 cm, u = 3.5 cm

INDEX

INDEX